CONTENTS

30 DAY VOCAL BOOTCAMP

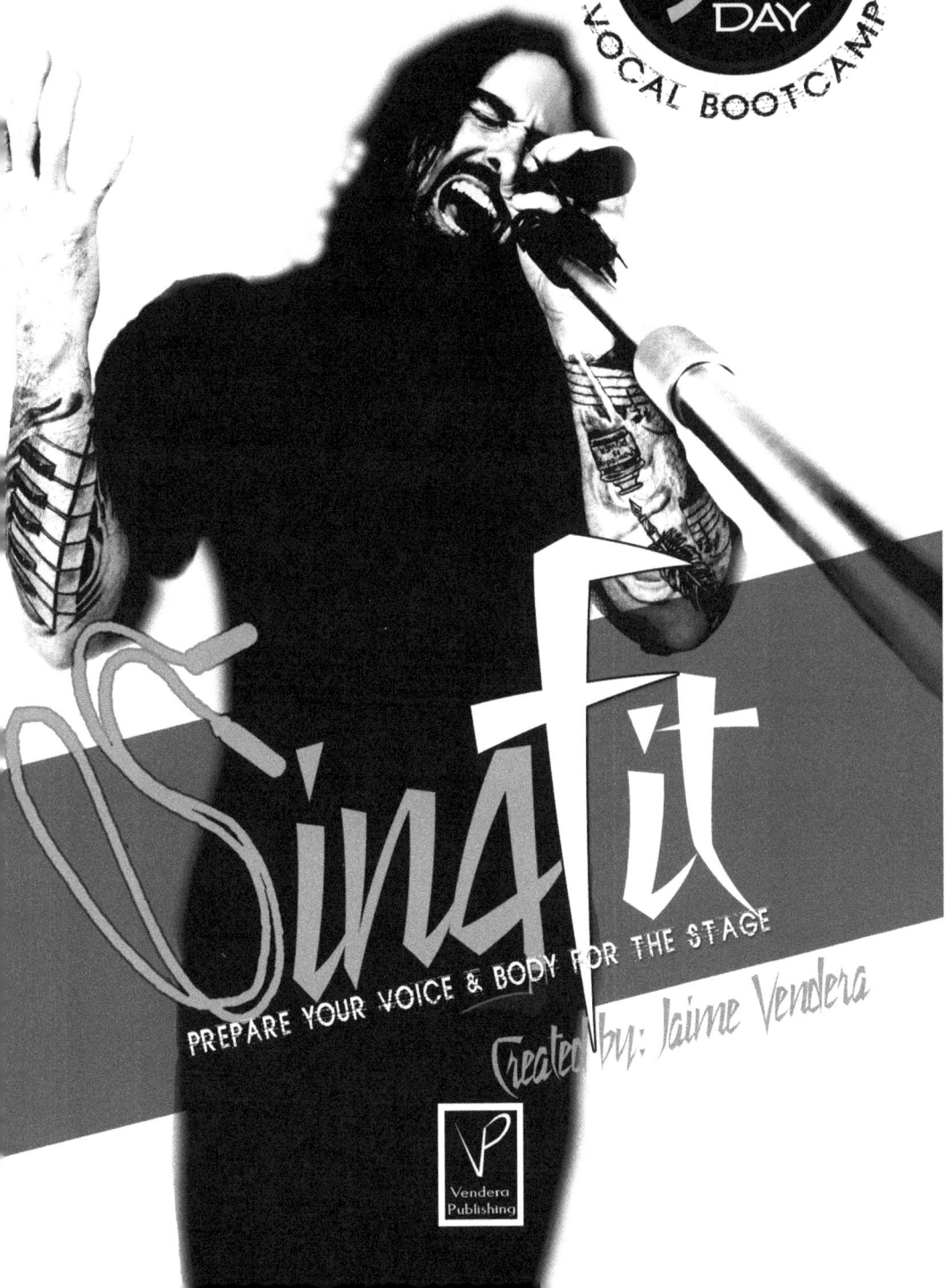

SingFit

PREPARE YOUR VOICE & BODY FOR THE STAGE

Created by: Jaime Vendera

Vendera Publishing

Interior Design: Daniel Middleton
www.scribefreelance.com

Cover Design: Molly Burnside
www.crosssidedesigns.com

Editor: Richard Dalglish

Photography: Sean Daniel
www.seandanielmedia.com

Bio Illustration: Genna Scheetz

Models featured in Interior photos: Carrie Vance and Ryan Waddell
Photographer: Justin Cotterell

ISBN: 978-1-936307-42-5

To access bonus SingFit material
Go to JaimeVendera.com/members
Click on "SingFit"
The password is "fittosing"

SINGFIT

BUILD A BETTER VOICE & BODY IN 30 DAYS.

Welcome to my latest book, *SingFit*. "SingFit" is a term I coined to refer to the act of singing or vocalizing while simultaneously performing physical exercises to strengthen both the voice and body. Studies have revealed the effects of cardiovascular exercise on singers and shown how exercises such as chin-ups affect the voice. SingFit covers all types of combinations of singing/vocalizing and exercising, from cardio to mass-building exercises and more. This particular SingFit program, which I've dubbed V30, is five full weeks of pure torture, with one rest day per week, which means you're looking at thirty hard-core days of vocal workouts and physical exercise. This unique program will start whipping you into rock-star shape vocally and physically in only 30 days. Who doesn't want to sound better AND look better on stage?

     V30 combines methods from my books *Raise Your Voice*, *Raise Your Voice 2: The Advanced Manual*, *Reclaim Your Voice*, *The Ultimate Breathing Workout*, and *Unleash Your Creative Mindset*. V30 will make you sweat, possibly even cry. But, if you complete the 30-Day Vocal Boot Camp, you'll be on your way to becoming vocally and physically ripped. Before long, you'll have fans begging to know your secrets for such an incredible voice—and, of course, that rockin' body!

     You may be wondering what possessed me to combine vocal exercise with physical exercise. Without even knowing, I've been a SingFit singer for years, cardio singing nearly every day by singing songs while jogging. Cardio singing does amazing things for vocal stamina, so I've always wondered if other forms of exercise might prove beneficial. Over the years, I've played with the idea of creating a 30-day SingFit-style vocal boot camp for singers. I decided the time for that boot camp was now, but I knew I'd have to develop it and test it for myself first.

When starting to develop a new SingFit program, I experimented with exercises like bench presses and squats while performing my Isolation exercises. After much experimentation, I discovered that the full-voice tones worked best, so I dropped Falsetto Slides and Transcending Tones and focused on full-voice Sirens during my workout. Over the course of several months, I shed some weight, regained some energy, and noticed that my mid-range was becoming stronger. The mid-range is the area right above the vocal break that proves most difficult for beginning singers. I've worked with many singers who have strong low voices and can wail on super-high notes, but shy away from that area right above their break for roughly five to seven notes.

The problematic mid-range is precisely why I introduced the stair-stepping method in *Raise Your Voice 2*—to strengthen those money notes, eliminate those weak spots. Though stair stepping is still effective and should be applied when you've plateaued, the Voice & Body Workout will take that mid-range to the next level while building your body!

In the pursuit of perfection, I continued fine-tuning the Voice & Body Workout, performing different exercises until I was satisfied with my routine. I had created a vocal workout/physical exercise routine that could be completed in under twenty minutes. But one day while bench-pressing, I had an epiphany. Free weights aren't always available, especially for touring singers, and many singers aren't focused on bulking up. I know I wasn't. So I decided to switch to bodyweight exercises like push-ups and sit-ups.

After several more weeks, I had another epiphany. Many singers complain that they seldom notice a significant difference in their voice as they perform vocal exercises. No wonder. Most singers barely squeak out a 10- to 15-minute vocal routine per day, if that, anxiously anticipating the last note of the last scale. FYI: You CAN notice a difference in less than twenty minutes, but you must hit it hard with an exercise like my Ultimate Isolation exercise. However, time wasn't an issue with the Voice & Body Workout, because the minutes flew by.

Bottom line: If you want a better voice, and a better body for that matter, it should NEVER be a race to the finish line; always take your time with your workouts. If you perform them properly, your voice should feel stronger and more resonant, like a flower opening to full bloom, by the time you've finished your vocal workout.

Since I could easily finish the Voice & Body Workout in way less than 20 minutes, I decided to double the exercise routine to extend it beyond the 20-minute mark. I had been performing five sets of Sirens, each set on a different vowel, while performing specific bodyweight exercises (push-ups, chin-ups, dips, squats, sit-ups, leg lifts, and torso twists), which turned into ten sets total for more vocal and physical exercise.

I was becoming proficient at performing this new routine, even at double the work (which actually wasn't double the time). So proficient, in fact, that I decided to add jump rope into the mix to get the heart rate up. I was now performing seven bodyweight exercises and jumping rope per each full-voice Siren set, for a total of ten sets. By the time I finished this unique SingFit routine, I was beat, but my voice and body felt great!

At first, I was unsure if my approach would fatigue my body if I did it six days per week. I was worried that I might go beyond the point of muscle recovery. It wasn't until filming vocal instructional videos for *Guitar Interactive Magazine* and discussing my V30 SingFit program with film producer Jamie Borden that it all made sense. A drummer in top physical shape, Jamie knows a lot about physical exercise. I shared my ideas with him, and his input helped to ease my concerns and solidify the routine. (Thanks, Jamie.)

Once I had perfected the Voice & Body Workout, it took me less than thirty minutes to perform the entire routine, which I always did first thing in the morning (which trains you to be ready to sing early in the day), including my Vocal Stress Release warm-up and my Voice & Body cool-down routines.

I had created an amazing routine. But, as the gears turned in my head, I envisioned my 30-day program for singers, and I knew the morning routine would not be enough training, especially if I wanted to go boot-camp style. Do you think that when you join the military, you head to boot camp, perform a hundred pushups, run a few miles, and your day is done? Absolutely not!

After much planning, I created a purely INSANE vocal boot camp by adding afternoon and evening routines consisting of other concepts from my books, including the Total Body Cardio routine, my Ultimate Breathing Workout exercises, non-vocal exercises such as Bullfrogs and Tongue Push-ups, the Ultimate Isolation exercise, and a round of cardio singing.

This program will NOT be easy, but if you're up to the challenge you'll be blown away by your results. Think of the V30 as the singer's version of P90X. I guarantee that this WILL be the hardest five workout weeks of your life. You'll be crying like a baby by the time your head hits your pillow, then sleeping like one. But eventually you'll be singing like an angel, screaming like a banshee, and looking like a chiseled Adonis. Not to fear, I've designed V30 to ease you into the program day by day until you're a V30 pro!

Are you up for the Vendera 30-day Vocal Boot Camp Challenge? Great! Simply follow each day of the daily diary in the back of this book, checking off each section as you finish it. Now clear your mind and say a prayer, because the pain is about to begin.

CHAPTER ONE
A BREAKDOWN OF V30

V30 has twelve steps. I'm assuming you're familiar with my vocal methodology and exercises. If not, you can learn how to perform the various exercises by studying my books *Raise Your Voice*, *Raise Your Voice 2: The Advanced Manual*, *The Ultimate Breathing Workout*, *Reclaim Your Voice*, and *Unleash Your Creative Mindset*. Here are the twelve steps:

V30 Boot Camp Steps

1. **Tabata Breathing.** Tabata breathing is covered in *Reclaim Your Voice/The Air & Water Diet*. This exercise is your metabolism primer to pump the lungs and energize your body before you start your morning routine.

2. **Mind/Body Process.** This body/mind meditation is covered in *Unleash Your Creative Mindset*. It's used to prepare your mind for your workout.

3. **Tibetan Five Rites.** This yoga warm-up awakens the body and is said to instill youthfulness. Though this step is optional, I highly recommend you include it in your routine.

4. **Vocal Stress Release/Vocal Stage Prep + Voice RX Warm-up.** Vocal Stress Release and Vocal Stage Prep are covered in *Raise Your Voice* and *Raise Your Voice 2*. The Voice RX warm-up is a 15-minute warm-up MP3 on lip bubbles, designed to get blood flowing to your vocal cords.

5. **Voice & Body Workout.** This is the ten-set routine vocalizing on Sirens while performing bodyweight exercises. Since this is my new concept, it is covered in this book. Sirens are explained in *Raise Your Voice* and *Raise Your Voice 2*.

6. **Voice & Body Cool-down.** This yoga stretching and vocalization cool-down stills the mind and caresses the vocal cords. It's covered in *Raise Your Voice 2*.

7. **Supplementation.** Supplementation will include increasing water intake, adding supplements to your daily regimen, and juice fasting on certain days to clear the body of mucus and boost the immune system.

8. **Total Body Cardio**. This bodyweight exercise is covered in *Raise Your Voice 2*. We slip Total Body Cardio into the afternoon session to get the muscles and lungs energized before beginning non-vocal and breathing exercises.

9. **Non-vocal Exercises.** Non-vocal exercises such as Bullfrogs are covered in *Raise Your Voice*. These exercises build the muscles that aid in vocal tone production and strain elimination.

10. **Breathing Exercises.** My breathing routine is covered in *The Ultimate Breathing Workout* and *Beyond the Ultimate Breathing Workout*. This program is designed to build a breathing core of steel.

11. **The Ultimate Isolation Exercise**. The Ultimate Isolation exercise warms and stretches the vocal cords. It is covered in *Raise Your Voice 2*.

12. **Cardio Singing.** Cardio singing is another SingFit concept, combining singing while running on a treadmill, jogging, or jumping on a rebounder. This concept is covered in *Raise Your Voice* and the *Sing Out Loud* series.

Before covering each step in detail, I'd like to share my V30 essentials list to assure a successful 30-day vocal training boot camp.

V30 Essentials
Items marked with an asterisk are optional. Here's your list:

1. My books *Raise Your Voice, Raise Your Voice 2, The Ultimate Breathing Workout, Reclaim Your Voice,* and *Unleash Your Creative Mindset.* Optional books include *The Ultimate Vocal Workout Diary* and *Superior Vocal Health.*

2. Water

3. *Water sachets (singerswater.com)

4. Yoga mat

5. Jump rope

6. Rebounder or treadmill

7. Broom or microphone stand

8. Chair or raised surface for dips

9. Chin-up bar

10. MP3 player

11. Pitch wheel or the TUNED XD singing app

12. *Sinus Clear Out (superiorvocalhealth.com)

13. *Vocal Eze (VocalEze.com)

14. *FoodScience of Vermont Aangamik® DMG

15. *Vega Sport Pre-Workout formula (vegasport.com)

16. Protein powder of your choice

17. Vitamin C powder such as Emergen-C

18. Liquid ionic zinc

19. Liquid chlorophyll

20. Colloidal silver

21. Braggs apple cider vinegar

22. Juicer

23. *Q-Link pendant (artistqlink.com)

These items are essential for your success in this vocal boot camp. Emergen-C, Braggs apple cider vinegar, DMG (thanks goes to David Katz, author of *Superior Vocal Health* for this suggestion), chlorophyll, colloidal silver, and zinc can be purchased through multiple online stores such as vitacost.com. If you want to know why each ingredient is important, please do a little research. I don't believe a detailed explanation of the "whys" is necessary here, but all these items help to boost immune response, muscle growth, etc. It sounds like a lot of supplies, but it really isn't. In fact, if you're one of my readers, you may already own half the list. Please purchase the required essential items before beginning V30.

DISCLAIMER: I am NOT a personal trainer nor am I an expert in physical exercise or nutrition. My approach is based on what I have found to work best for me to improve my voice and body, and I've kept the descriptions as simple as possible so I don't bore you by naming muscle groups, explaining why one exercise works better than another, etc. Therefore, the following sections are not intended to prescribe, treat, prevent, or diagnose any illness. Consult with your physician before attempting the following exercises and before taking any of the products, vitamins, minerals, or herbs listed in this book.

Now let's move on to the next chapter to review each step.

CHAPTER TWO
THE TWELVE STEPS

The twelve steps are broken down into segments to be performed throughout the day, morning, afternoon, and night. Following is a basic guide for each step.

MORNING WORKOUT

Your morning workout will be the toughest, but it's an excellent way to train your voice to be ready to sing as soon as the sunrise brightens the morning. Here we go:

Step One: Tabata Breathing

This four-minute exercise is your oxygen primer. It is explained in *The Air & Water Diet*, which is also available in *Reclaim Your Voice*. Perform one four-minute set of Tabata breathing as soon as you wake up. You can use the Tabata Timer on the TUNED XD app.

Step Two: The Mind/Body Process

This step is explained in *Unleash Your Creative Mindset*. It is your mental primer. It will spark your creative genius and help end procrastination, which is helpful for mornings when you don't feel like exercising. The Mind/Body Process automatically prepares the subconscious mind to flood with successful thoughts. After you finish this step, and before starting your hard-core morning exercise routine, take three squirts of Vocal Eze directly into the mouth, followed by 16 ounces of water with one dropperful of Sinus Clear Out, one dropperful of DGM, and one scoop of Vega Sport.

Step Three: Tibetan Five Rites

The Tibetan five rites of rejuvenation are a series of five yoga exercises that energize the body. Though this step is optional, I truly believe the Five Rites will help to keep you looking and feeling youthful, especially on stage.

Each rite is performed 21 times (or 21 repetitions). Follow the daily planner and you'll slowly grow from one rep per rite per day, to the full 21 reps per rite per day. Here is a breakdown on how to perform each rite:

Rite #1. Stand up straight with your arms at your sides, perpendicular to the floor, palms toward the floor. Begin to spin clockwise. Inhale and exhale normally. Never hold your breath. It helps to find a focus point such as a picture on the wall, a clock, etc., to bring your attention to with each spin. Otherwise, you might become dizzy. Each complete spin equals one rep.

Rite #2. Lie on the floor on your back with your arms at your sides and against your body, palms pressed against the floor. Raise your head off the floor, bringing your chin to your chest as you simultaneously lift your legs straight up off the floor until your feet are pointed toward the ceiling. Keep your legs straight. Breathe in deeply as you lift your head and legs and exhale as you return your head and legs to the floor to complete one rep.

Rite #3. Kneel on the floor while placing your hands on the back of your thighs. Your toes should be pressing against the floor. Drop your chin to your chest. Inhale deeply as you stretch the neck back and arch the spine. Exhale as you return your body to a straight position and your chin back to your chest to complete one rep.

Rite #4. Sit on the floor with your legs straight out in front of you, approximately twelve inches apart, with your hands at your sides, palms pressed against the floor. Allow your head to fall forward so that the chin touches the chest. As you inhale deeply, raise the body to form a table out of your torso with your legs and arms acting as the table legs. Allow your head to drop back. Exhale as you return to the sitting position to complete one rep.

Rite #5. Lie face down on the floor with your palms placed on the floor at your sides and your elbows bent. As you inhale deeply, raise your buttocks off the floor, with your arms and legs straightening until they're locked and your body forms an inverted V. As you exhale, lower your body as you begin to arch your back by extending your arms straight so that your head curls toward the ceiling to complete one rep.

Note: There are multiple videos online on sites such as YouTube that demonstrate how to perform each rite.

Step Four: Vocal Stress Release/Vocal Stage Prep + Voice RX Warm-up

Vocal Stress Release (VSR) and Vocal Stage Prep (VSP) are explained in *Raise Your Voice* and *Raise Your Voice 2. Beyond the Ultimate Vocal Warm Up* features a video demonstration of Vocal Stress Release. The member's section of *Raise Your Voice 2* contains a cheat sheet that combines VSR and VSP. The *Voice RX* warm-up MP3 is available for free at jaimevendera.com.

Step Five: The Voice & Body Workout

Ah, time for the meat of the program, the mid-range strengthener and body toner. Here's the breakdown of the Voice & Body Workout:

Physical Exercises

The exercises described below are to be performed in the exact order presented while vocalizing on Sirens, as explained in your vocal boot camp diary. The Voice & Body Workout—what I call the "bodyweight routine"—comprises eight bodyweight exercises. You will perform ten sets of the bodyweight routine, one set per vocal exercise.

Push-ups. Lying face down on the floor, with your back straight, place your palms on the floor at your sides with elbows tucked and pointing away from the body. Push your body up off the floor while maintaining a straight line down the back, fully extending your arms at the top. Make sure to keep your hands directly under your shoulders, NOT in front of your shoulders, in order to work the chest muscles. When pushing up, focus on creating an inward tension, as if you are trying to slide the palms together. This will further engage the chest muscles. Each time you push off the floor, you must silently count in your mind, "1 chest, 2 chest, 3 chest ..." for each rep, to direct the majority of the physical effort toward working the chest (pectoral) muscles instead of the arms. Mentally repeating the name of the muscle brings more mental energy to that area, which is key to quicker development. Lower your body back to the floor until the chest touches to complete one rep.

Chin-ups. In this system, I focus on chin-ups, not pull-ups. Grab the chin-up bar with your palms facing toward you. Start each chin-up with the body free hanging, feet off the floor. Slowly lift the body until your chin is above the bar. Chin-ups, which work the biceps and, more importantly, the back muscles, are extremely difficult, so do not be discouraged if you have trouble completing a full chin-up. Focus on lifting yourself as high as possible while silently counting, "1 back, 2 back, etc.," to engage the back muscles to perform the majority of the lifting. Hold at the top for a brief second before lowering yourself back down to complete one rep.

Dips. Place your hands to your sides and grasp the end of a chair or raised surface behind you. Extend your legs and lock them into position. Begin by dropping your body toward the floor until your triceps and forearms have formed a 90-degree angle. Lift yourself back up, locking the arms straight at the top to complete one rep. Mentally count, "1 arms, 2 arms, etc.," for each rep. You'll feel this exercise burning the triceps. That's the goal.

Sit-ups/Leg Lifts. This combo exercise is slightly different from the regular sit-up because it works the entire abdominal wall and lower back. Begin by lying with your back on the floor and your hands behind your head. Slowly roll the body upward, one vertebra at a time, as you bring your arms up into the air and lift your torso into a full sit-up position. Continue bending forward until your hands touch your toes. Slowly roll back down and drop your hands flat to your sides, parallel with your legs, until you are once again flat on the floor. Next, raise your legs up off the floor, using your palms for support until your toes are pointed toward the ceiling. At this point, roll your pelvis up off the floor to engage the lower abdominals. Lower your pelvis back to the floor and lower your legs back down flat on the floor as you raise your hands behind your head until they are once again lying on the floor behind you. Once your legs and arms are flat, you've resumed the beginning position and finished one rep.

It may seem awkward dropping the hands to the sides for the leg lifts instead of extending them behind your head. But the hands play an important part in protecting the lower back as you lift. Moreover, this will force the lower abdominals to do more work. You will feel a tighter burn in your abdominals with your hands at your sides. Also, do NOT begin to lift your legs into the leg lifts until your back is flat on the floor from the sit-up. It feels easier to begin bringing the legs up before you're flat on the floor, but this will not fully engage the lower abdominals. All through this exercise, remember to silently count, "1 core, 2 core, etc.," to focus the energy into the core of your abdominals. If you prefer to count twice per each rep, one count for the sit-up and one count for the leg lifts, such as "1 core, 1 core, 2 core, 2 core, etc.," it is fine.

Squats. Time to build those leg muscles and tighten up that rock star butt! Stand straight, feet shoulder-width apart, with hands straight out in front of you or placed on your hips. Lower your body while keeping your head straight and allowing the butt to move backwards as you bend at the knees. Keep your back straight and chest slightly puffed out to keep the spine aligned. Allow your thighs to become parallel to the floor at the bottom of the squat. If you are very flexible, you can go lower. Slowly raise back up to a standing position to complete one rep. Silently count, "1 legs, 2 legs, etc.," during this exercise. DO NOT flare out your knees as you squat. Keep your legs straight to protect the back and fully engage your thigh muscles.

Torso Twists. Torso twists work the abdominals, oblique muscles, and intercostal muscles. This little exercise will eliminate those love handles. Begin by placing a broom or microphone stand behind your neck across your shoulders. Keep your arms spread wide apart and slightly bend your knees. Twist slowly to one side, while keeping your head forward, and then twist to the opposite side to complete one rep. Think, "1 sides, 2 sides, etc.," to focus on all muscles involved. You may wish to repeat the count twice, once for each left and each right twist. If you tighten your abdominals, you will further engage the abdominal muscles for core development as well.

Jump rope. A jump rope will get you stage-stamina ready! It's best if you have a skip counter for jumping rope so you do not lose count or forget to vocalize on your Sirens. In addition, your rope needs to be the proper length. If you are five feet tall or under, use a seven-foot jump rope. Add one foot of rope for every additional six inches of height. With your feet shoulder-width apart, each handle gripped firmly, and the jump rope behind you, begin to spin the rope forward, making small circles with your wrists as you jump rope. Lift the feet together with each jump and only jump high enough to clear the rope. Keep in mind the rope should softly scrape the ground, which is easier when you keep the legs and torso relaxed, not rigid. Always lift from and land on the balls of your feet. As you progress, you can add weight to the handles, change direction by spinning the rope backward, even switch to jumping rope one foot at a time, like jogging in place.

Once you complete each set of the bodyweight routine, you can rest as you finish each Siren set (if you've finished the physical exercise first). At the end of each vocal exercise, take a large sip of water. I prefer the "gargle and slurp." I take a gulp of water, hold it in my mouth, tilt my head back to gargle, and then tilt my head forward, forming a tight "o" shape with my lips as I inhale as if I'm sipping through a straw. The gargle and slurp helps moisten the interior of the mouth and pulls water molecules down the trachea to coat the vocal cords. After each gargle and slurp, I swallow my water. Now that you have a grasp of each exercise, it's time to revisit our Sirens.

Note: You may lose track of your count for each exercise, which is one reason I use a skip counter for jumping rope. I personally picture the number of reps on my mind monitor (described in *Unleash Your Creative Mindset*) to keep track of my reps. Nevertheless, I know how easy it is to lose count, so I keep track of my reps by counting on my fingers. As I complete a rep, I slightly wiggle one finger at a time—right hand pointer, middle, ring, pinky, thumb, and then left hand pointer, middle, ring, pinky, thumb to count to ten. It is easier to remember 10, 20, 30, etc., but 1 through 9 can get muddled while vocalizing. Don't be afraid to count with your fingers, like you did when you were a child, to keep track of your reps.

Vocal Exercises

The Voice & Body Workout vocal exercises are always full-voice Sirens, maintaining a clear, clean, resonant tone on the same volume from the lowest note to the highest note, performed on various vowels and vowel combinations covering thirds, fifths, and octave slides. Refer to each day of your vocal boot camp diary for the correct vowel and exercise variation. If you've studied my method, you already understand how to perform these simple slides. However, for guidance you will be required to record versions of each type of mini-Siren, as explained later in this book. You can use TUNED XD to perform the pre-programmed SingFit V30 scales.

Step Six: Voice & Body Cool Down

After you've completed your Voice & Body Workout, you must cool down with the Voice & Body Cool Down, which is described in *Raise Your Voice 2*. You'll also use the Voice & Body Cool Down after cardio singing.

Step Seven: Supplementation

Always supplement in the morning. Remember, before your workout, take three squirts of Vocal Eze directly into the mouth, followed by a mix of one dropperful each of Sinus Clear Out and DMG with one scoop of Vega Sport pre-workout mix in a glass of water. This regimen will open the sinuses, feed the voice, and help the body take in more oxygen during your workout. Make sure to have plenty of water during your workout. I prefer hot water in a thermos. Hot water reduces vocal cord swelling and makes the voice feel wetter. Throughout the day, drink room-temperature water infused with water sachets from singerswater.com.

You are not required to use the water sachets or Vocal Eze, or drink the DMG/Vegasport/Sinus Clear Out mix, but they will enhance the quality of your workout and improve vocal health. Many people use stimulants such as caffeine, but this attacks the nervous system. Thanks to David Katz of Superior Vocal Health, I learned that DMG is a much wiser alternative to ramping up for an effective workout. If you suffer from caffeine addiction or any other addiction, such as smoking, refer to my *Vocal Reset*, available in *Reclaim Your Voice*, to help eliminate voice-diminishing habits from your life. Your 30-day vocal boot camp is the perfect time to become smoke-

and caffeine-free.

After your workout, eat your preferred breakfast. You can add glass of Voice Juice (which is similar to the Vocalade recipe from VenderaVocalAcademy.com) to your morning meal:

Voice Juice
*Eight to sixteen ounces of water
*One to two scoops of your preferred protein powder
*Half teaspoon of Bragg's apple cider vinegar (optional)
*Ten drops of liquid zinc
*One dropperful of colloidal silver
*One packet of Emergen-C or Crew Brew
*Two to three tablespoons of liquid chlorophyll

Apple cider vinegar is optional because it may make your Voice Juice taste too bitter. But ACV is an excellent source of vitamins and minerals that can boost your immune system, and it also helps prevent heartburn. At minimum, you should consider sipping a half-cup of warm water with a tablespoon each of apple cider vinegar and organic honey before every meal to aid digestion.

Notes for Morning Workout
You should begin your morning routine as early as possible, preferably 5 a.m. to 6 a.m. The earlier you start, the less likely you are to procrastinate. If I start when it's still dark, I flow through my routine. When I see the sun rising, I begin to rush because my mind drifts to daily tasks. Don't stress if you can't complete each rep for each exercise. Over time you will hit all your workout reps and goals. Always drink water with your workouts to hydrate the voice and body.

AFTERNOON WORKOUT
The afternoon workout focuses on non-vocal and breathing exercises. Here we go:

Step Eight: Total Body Cardio

Total Body Cardio is explained in detail in *Raise Your Voice 2*. This bodyweight exercise is an overall body primer before beginning your exercises.

Step Nine: Non-Vocal Exercises

Non-vocal exercises are covered in *Raise Your Voice*. Follow your practice guide and refer to *Raise Your Voice* to know which exercises to perform each day and how to perform each exercise.

Step Ten: The Ultimate Breathing Workout

This nine-step breathing exercise routine is covered in my book *The Ultimate Breathing Workout* and demonstrated in the video *Beyond the Ultimate Breathing Workout*. Do not perform the advanced breathing (Applied Breathing Isometrics, Breath Builders), as the advanced breathing exercises should only be added after you've completed your first five-week vocal boot camp.

Notes for Afternoon Workout

Your afternoon workout can be completed in as little as fifteen minutes. However, do NOT rush the exercises. Do not hold or lock your breath. Keep a daily diary, especially for the breathing workout. Either write down the names of the exercises in a notebook and list your daily times, or you can use *The Ultimate Vocal Workout Diary*.

EVENING WORKOUT

Your evening workout is designed to get you singing, though we'll begin with vocal exercise to warm up and stretch the cords. Please note: You CAN sing throughout the day. You are not limited to singing only at night.

Step Eleven: The Ultimate IsolationExercise

The Voice & Body Workout focuses on strengthening the full voice mid-range, while the Ultimate Isolation exercise works the lower, mid, and upper range in falsetto and full voice. Refer to *Raise Your Voice 2* and my *Beyond the Voice* video series for exercise instructions. In addition, note your daily range in the *Ultimate Vocal Workout Diary*. Follow the boot camp diary, because we'll be switching from dynamically soft to dynamically loud.

Step Twelve: Cardio Singing

Cardio singing works the lungs, abdominals, and intercostal muscles as you focus on vocal technique. It's a great way to build stage stamina. Follow the daily vocal boot camp diary in order to know how many songs to sing per night and how to sing them. Choose comfortable songs for your current range. As your voice grows, you can add more-difficult songs. You can jog, jump on a rebounder, ride a bike, or run on a treadmill.

Notes for Evening Workout

Start the Ultimate Isolation exercise higher than usual. Males who start this exercise on C4 below the typical break should begin above the break on an F4. Females who start on F4 below the typical break should start on A4, below Tenor C5, to place the voice right above the typical break. Work both upscale and downscale on a vowel per day as listed in the daily vocal boot camp diary. Make sure to read each section of the daily vocal boot camp diary to perform each step/exercise correctly and cardio sing with the correct tone, at the correct volume, for the correct length of time.

That's my SingFit V30 insane vocal boot camp program in a nutshell. Just remember to focus on your vocal technique. Additionally, sustain your slides. Do not cut them short and do not forget to vocalize as you're silently counting. Drink plenty of water and remember the gargle and slurp. A lot of success comes from the mental mindset. Feel free to keep your Mindset Diary as you start V30. Use positive mantras throughout your day and as you perform each vocal boot camp session. I often repeat, "Voice but Stronger." It is my personal mantra and motto, because I can build your voice, but stronger than you've ever imagined. Pick a mantra and stick with it.

Before beginning your first day of vocal boot camp, review my books and make sure you have all the essential tools you need to start this program. When you dare to begin, flip to the next page.

CHAPTER THREE
V30 DAY BY DAY

I was going to line this program out in the *Ultimate Vocal Workout Diary* because that's what I used to keep track of my daily V30 routine during this adventure. But, for the sake of simplicity, I decided to present the entire program in this book so all you'd have to do is follow each day, checking off each step as you complete it. PLEASE do not skip a day or a session. If you do, even if it's simply that you forgot to do the afternoon session, you'll need to repeat the entire day. You can adjust the starting times during the day for when each section is performed, but you MUST complete all three sections every day.

You may want to keep using your *Ultimate Vocal Workout Diary*, especially for tracking your breathing exercises and highest pitch for the Ultimate Isolation exercise, as well as for listing your cardio singing song list. Above all, don't forget your vocal technique:

1. For each exercise, keep ALL your tones clean and clear and at the correct volume, whether soft or loud.

2. Breathe low as you inhale to fill the tank.

3. Support low. (Add more gas/downward support as needed.)

4. Focus your voice up into the palate.

5. Maintain correct facial positions for each vowel, as explained in *Raise Your Voice 2*.

6. You must turn the head side to side for the "NO" movement whenever you begin to feel vocal strain. Your chin must line up with the right shoulder when turning the head right and left shoulder when turning the head left. The "NO" should be continual and somewhat fast, like the your car's windshield wipers working side to side in a downpour. If using the "NO,"

do NOT allow your head to stop moving side to side. If you do, it is a sign of external neck tension.

7. When working into your mid-range and beyond, remember the "Sean Connery" or "Dr. Evil" voice to narrow the palate and create the teepee in the roof of your mouth as described in *Raise Your Voice 2*.

8. Perform each exercise slowly.

9. Drink plenty of water between each exercise. Remember, singers need a LOT of water all day long!

10. NEVER hold your breath!

Now you're ready to tackle the V30 vocal boot camp. Follow along each day, checking off each box as it is completed, and in five weeks you'll be a vocal machine! Let us begin.

WEEK 1

This first week, we'll ease you into the program, performing only 20% of the total reps per set of the bodyweight routine in the morning. Each set consists of the following:

Push-ups: 2 reps
Chin-ups: 1 rep
Triceps dips: 2 reps
Sit-ups into leg lifts: 2 reps
Squats: 4 reps
Torso twists: 2 reps
Jump rope: 10 reps

If you think 2-1-2-2-4-2-10 as you work through each set of the bodyweight routine, you won't forget your reps per exercise. You MUST perform the bodyweight routine ten times, one set per vocal exercise. This first week may seem easy, as if you aren't benefiting from the physical workout. Don't underestimate this system. I start with minimum reps to ease you into the program and prepare you for the more difficult weeks to come. If you finish your bodyweight routine before a vocal exercise is complete, use the additional time to rest until you've finished the vocal exercise and can start your routine again for the next vocal exercise.

For Week 1, our goal is to vocalize over one full octave by performing mini-Sirens on thirds, starting down one octave and working up to the first note below your vocal break. That means you will start your initial pitch, slide slowly up one third, work up the scale in half-step increments until you reach one half-step below your vocal break, and then return to your beginning pitch.

FYI: The note that is an octave below one-half step below your vocal break will be your point of reference throughout the V30 SingFit program. You may recall from *Raise Your Voice* that our point of reference is a note at which we start all of our exercises. Typically, it is C4 (middle C) for males and F4 (F above middle C) for females. But this is not necessarily the case in this program, as our SingFit point of reference will depend on one's natural vocal range and will start an octave lower.

Since the vocal exercises in the Voice & Body Workout are designed to be perfectly matched to each singer's range, we must first discover where your natural vocal break occurs. Though many males break on an E4 or the E above middle C (C4), and many women break on an A4, or the A below tenor C (C5), this is not always the case. To find your break, begin vocalizing on a YAY on your lowest note and slowly slide up the scale as high as you can go until you feel or hear an area that naturally wants to flip or crack. This may be difficult if you are a user of my methods, because you have possibly learned to smooth out the break. If this is the case, refer to your *Ultimate Vocal Workout Diary* to review the very first day you began using the Isolation method to recall where your break occurred. My break occurred at an E4.

During Week 1, we do not want to cross the break, only work up to right below it. Here's the hard part. You will have to record your own Sirens to match your voice. The recording doesn't have to be a professional production. You can do this with a handheld recorder, even with your smart phone. Simply record yourself playing mini-Sirens on a guitar or piano playing the beginning note, then top, then beginning note as described in each day of the V30 diary. During the morning workout, you will not be able to use a pitch wheel due to your bodyweight routine. You'll need to record ten versions, to be played one after another if you wish to sing along to the correct vowel patterns, OR you can simply record one mini-Siren set without vocals and set that one scale on your MP3 player to repeat.

Note: A better alternative is to use my TUNED XD application, which features a scale generator, as well as the SingFit V30 scales pre-programmed into the app. You can set the range of the scale and speed to match your voice. If the number behind a note (e.g., C4, E4, etc.) is confusing, note that the "4" simply refers to the fourth octave on a piano. You can also use TUNED XD to hear the actual pitch for C1–C7.

Your goal for the mini-Sirens in the first week is to attempt to cover one octave. Since my break point originally occurred at an E4, my highest note that I want to work up to is D#4, which means that my V30 SingFit point of reference is actually D#3. To incorporate a slide up a major third to my point of reference, I started my scales on a B2, sliding up to D#3 and back down to B2, and worked up step by step to cover one octave, ending on B3-D#4-B3. For females typically breaking at A4, I recorded mini-Sirens on thirds, beginning at E3-G#3-E3 (or 1-3-1), and working up an octave to E4-G#4-E4. YES, this might feel too low on the first few mini-Sirens, especially for females, but attempt to reach those lowest notes. We want to both strengthen and expand our lowest notes as well as our high notes.

For each vocal exercise, the first five sets will consist of the individual vowels YAH, YAY, YEE, YOH, and YOU. I always begin the vowel with a "Y" to prevent breathiness and glottal shock. The second set of five vocal exercises requires you to modify the vowels as you slide up and down. Each vowel modification is explained in your daily vocal boot camp diary.

Also, I am issuing a "Two-Gallon-**Minimum** Water Challenge" for males and "One-Gallon-**Minimum** Water Challenge" for females, which means it's time to up your water intake. Yes, in *Raise Your Voice* I present a water formula, and this challenge may seem to double your usual water intake, but you are now working out extremely hard and losing body fluid, which you must replenish. You MUST drink LOTS of water throughout the day, especially during each workout session. Let's begin Day One.

DAY 1

MORNING ROUTINE

Start time between 5:00 AM-7:00 AM

Tabata Breathing	☐
Mind/Body Process	☐
16-ounce water mixture (SVH + DMG)	☐
Five Rites- One rep each	☐
VSR/VSP/Voice RX Warm up	☐

Sirens 1-3-1

YAH + bodyweight routine	☐
YAY + bodyweight routine	☐
YEE + bodyweight routine	☐
YOH + bodyweight routine	☐
YOU + bodyweight routine	☐
YAH-AY-AH + bodyweight routine	☐
YAY-EE-AY + bodyweight routine	☐
YEE-OH-EE + bodyweight routine	☐
YOH-OU-OH + bodyweight routine	☐
YOU-AH-OU + bodyweight routine	☐
Voice & Body Cool Down	☐

Voice Juice	☐

DAY 1

AFTERNOON ROUTINE

Start time between 12:00PM-5:00PM

Total Body Cardio- One set   ☐
Ultimate Breathing Workout   ☐
Bullfrogs- 20 reps   ☐
Tongue Pushups- 20 reps   ☐

EVENING ROUTINE

60-90 minutes before bedtime

Ultimate Isolation Exercise (Dynamically soft on YAH)   ☐
Cardio singing- Sing two songs on lip bubbles   ☐
Voice & Body Cool Down   ☐

DAY 2

MORNING ROUTINE

Start time between 5:00 AM-7:00 AM

Tabata Breathing ☐
Mind/Body Process ☐
16-ounce water mixture (SVH + DMG) ☐
Five Rites- Two reps each ☐
VSR/VSP/Voice RX Warm up ☐

Sirens 1-3-1
YAH + bodyweight routine ☐
YAY + bodyweight routine ☐
YEE + bodyweight routine ☐
YOH + bodyweight routine ☐
YOU + bodyweight routine ☐
YAH-AY-AH + bodyweight routine ☐
YAY-EE-AY + bodyweight routine ☐
YEE-OH-EE + bodyweight routine ☐
YOH-OU-OH + bodyweight routine ☐
YOU-AH-OU + bodyweight routine ☐
Voice & Body Cool Down ☐

Voice Juice ☐

DAY 2

AFTERNOON ROUTINE

Start time between 12:00PM-5:00PM

Total Body Cardio- One set ☐
Ultimate Breathing Workout ☐
Platysma Pull ups- 10 reps ☐
Head Curls- 10 reps front and back ☐

EVENING ROUTINE

60-90 minutes before bedtime

Ultimate Isolation Exercise (Dynamically soft on YAY) ☐
Cardio singing- Sing two songs while humming (mmm) ☐
Voice & Body Cool Down ☐

DAY 3

MORNING ROUTINE

Start time between 5:00 AM-7:00 AM

Tabata Breathing ☐
Mind/Body Process ☐
16-ounce water mixture (SVH + DMG) ☐
Five Rites- Three reps each ☐
VSR/VSP/Voice RX Warm up ☐

Sirens 1-3-1
YAH + bodyweight routine ☐
YAY + bodyweight routine ☐
YEE + bodyweight routine ☐
YOH + bodyweight routine ☐
YOU + bodyweight routine ☐
YAH-AY-AH + bodyweight routine ☐
YAY-EE-AY + bodyweight routine ☐
YEE-OH-EE + bodyweight routine ☐
YOH-OU-OH + bodyweight routine ☐
YOU-AH-OU + bodyweight routine ☐
Voice & Body Cool Down ☐

Voice Juice ☐

DAY 3

AFTERNOON ROUTINE

Start time between 12:00PM-5:00PM

Total Body Cardio- One set ☐
Ultimate Breathing Workout ☐
Bullfrogs- 20 reps ☐
Tongue Pushups- 20 reps ☐

EVENING ROUTINE

60-90 minutes before bedtime

Ultimate Isolation Exercise (Dynamically soft on YEE) ☐
Cardio singing- Sing two songs at low volume ☐
Voice & Body Cool Down ☐

DAY 4

MORNING ROUTINE

Start time between 5:00 AM-7:00 AM

Tabata Breathing ☐
Mind/Body Process ☐
16-ounce water mixture (SVH + DMG) ☐
Five Rites- Four reps each ☐
VSR/VSP/Voice RX Warm up ☐

Sirens 1-3-1
YAH + bodyweight routine ☐
YAY + bodyweight routine ☐
YEE + bodyweight routine ☐
YOH + bodyweight routine ☐
YOU + bodyweight routine ☐
YAH-AY-AH + bodyweight routine ☐
YAY-EE-AY + bodyweight routine ☐
YEE-OH-EE + bodyweight routine ☐
YOH-OU-OH + bodyweight routine ☐
YOU-AH-OU + bodyweight routine ☐
Voice & Body Cool Down ☐

Voice Juice ☐

DAY 4

AFTERNOON ROUTINE

Start time between 12:00PM-5:00PM

Total Body Cardio- One set   ☐
Ultimate Breathing Workout   ☐
Platysma Pullups- 10 reps   ☐
Head Curls- 10 reps front and back   ☐

EVENING ROUTINE

60-90 minutes before bedtime

Ultimate Isolation Exercise (Dynamically soft on YOH)   ☐
Cardio singing- Sing two songs at medium volume   ☐
Voice & Body Cool Down   ☐

DAY 5

MORNING ROUTINE

Start time between 5:00 AM-7:00 AM

Tabata Breathing   ☐
Mind/Body Process   ☐
16-ounce water mixture (SVH + DMG)   ☐
Five Rites- Five reps each   ☐
VSR/VSP/Voice RX Warm up   ☐

Sirens 1-3-1
YAH + bodyweight routine   ☐
YAY + bodyweight routine   ☐
YEE + bodyweight routine   ☐
YOH + bodyweight routine   ☐
YOU + bodyweight routine   ☐
YAH-AY-AH + bodyweight routine   ☐
YAY-EE-AY + bodyweight routine   ☐
YEE-OH-EE + bodyweight routine   ☐
YOH-OU-OH + bodyweight routine   ☐
YOU-AH-OU + bodyweight routine   ☐
Voice & Body Cool Down   ☐

Voice Juice   ☐

DAY 5

AFTERNOON ROUTINE

Start time between 12:00PM-5:00PM

Total Body Cardio- One set ☐
Ultimate Breathing Workout ☐
Bullfrogs- 20 reps ☐
Tongue Pushups- 20 reps ☐

EVENING ROUTINE

60-90 minutes before bedtime

Ultimate Isolation Exercise (Dynamically soft on YOU) ☐
Cardio singing- Sing two songs at full volume ☐
Voice & Body Cool Down ☐

DAY 6

MORNING ROUTINE

Start time between 5:00 AM-7:00 AM

Tabata Breathing ☐
Mind/Body Process ☐
16-ounce water mixture (SVH + DMG) ☐
Five Rites- Six reps each ☐
VSR/VSP/Voice RX Warm up ☐

Sirens 1-3-1
YAH + bodyweight routine ☐
YAY + bodyweight routine ☐
YEE + bodyweight routine ☐
YOH + bodyweight routine ☐
YOU + bodyweight routine ☐
YAH-AY-AH + bodyweight routine ☐
YAY-EE-AY + bodyweight routine ☐
YEE-OH-EE + bodyweight routine ☐
YOH-OU-OH + bodyweight routine ☐
YOU-AH-OU + bodyweight routine ☐
Voice & Body Cool Down ☐

Voice Juice ☐

DAY 6

AFTERNOON ROUTINE

Start time between 12:00PM-5:00PM

Total Body Cardio- One set ☐
Ultimate Breathing Workout ☐
Platysma Pull ups- 10 reps ☐
Head Curls- 10 reps front and back ☐

EVENING ROUTINE

60-90 minutes before bedtime

Ultimate Isolation Exercise (Dynamically loud on YAH) ☐
Cardio singing- Sing two songs at full volume ☐
Voice & Body Cool Down ☐

REST DAY

Today you deserve a vocal break! Don't get too excited, because it isn't a total break. You must still warm up your voice for the day. Start your morning off with Vocal Stress Release/Vocal Stage Prep while singing along to *Voice RX*. You'll feel better if you do your warm-up routine while in the shower, because the hot water relaxes the body, and the steam will open the sinuses and moisturize the vocal cords. Afterwards, drink one cup of the Voice Juice. Sing throughout the day if you feel the desire.

Today you enter the world of juice fasting! Nothing but juice this entire day! After your cup of Voice Juice, you can choose from a variety of juice mixes to drink. I like to juice six to eight leaves of kale, four carrots, two apples, two stalks of celery, one cucumber, and a small chunk of ginger. Bottom line, relax today and sip up. Why are we juicing? To give your digestive system a break and to shake some of the slag from your system. Juice fasting will energize you! There is nothing worse than a lethargic singer, ha-ha. Furthermore, I'm trying to get you interested in fruits and veggies, as they do the singer's body good. There is more on diet and juicing in the books *Raise Your Voice* and *Superior Vocal Health*, if you're interested in changing your eating lifestyle.

WEEK 2

During the second week we'll increase our reps to 40% of total reps per each set of the bodyweight routine in the morning. Each set now consists of the following:

Push-ups: 4 reps
Chin-ups: 2 reps
Triceps dips: 4 reps
Sit-ups into leg lifts: 4 reps
Squats: 8 reps
Torso twists: 4 reps
Jump rope: 20 reps

Remember, 4-2-4-4-8-4-20. In addition, we're switching from thirds to fifths on our Sirens. It's also time to move the ending pitch up by two steps to place us right above our break. For males with a typical break at E4, we're now working up to F4 as opposed to D#4 from last week, although we maintain our initial point of reference. Females with a typical break point of A4 will now work up to A#4 instead of G#4 from last week. For fifths, we start a bit lower to cover the fifth slide. Males would start at G#2-D#3-G#2 (or 1-5-1), working up to A#3-F4-A#3. Females would start C#3-G#3-C#3, working up an octave to D#4-A#4-D#4. Please be aware that these notes might feel extremely low, especially for many females. If you find that Week 2 has you vocalizing too low for your voice (based on your vocal break), adjust the TUNED XD SingFit scales accordingly. This might result in fewer scale patterns, which means you may complete the scale before the bodyweight exercises, but that is fine as long as both are completed.

This is why it is better for you to record your own scales, OR, use TUNED XD. Stick with it; in time, your lower range will expand. Regardless, do not go past the top note set for this week. If your break doesn't occur at E4 (males) or A4 (females) adjust the top note up or down accordingly.

DAY 1

MORNING ROUTINE

Start time between 5:00 AM-7:00 AM

Tabata Breathing ☐
Mind/Body Process ☐
16-ounce water mixture (SVH + DMG) ☐
Five Rites- Seven reps each ☐
VSR/VSP/Voice RX Warm up ☐

Sirens 1-5-1
YAH + bodyweight routine ☐
YAY + bodyweight routine ☐
YEE + bodyweight routine ☐
YOH + bodyweight routine ☐
YOU + bodyweight routine ☐
YAH-AY-AH + bodyweight routine ☐
YAY-EE-AY + bodyweight routine ☐
YEE-OH-EE + bodyweight routine ☐
YOH-OU-OH + bodyweight routine ☐
YOU-AH-OU + bodyweight routine ☐
Voice & Body Cool Down ☐

Voice Juice ☐

DAY 1

AFTERNOON ROUTINE

Start time between 12:00PM-5:00PM

Total Body Cardio- Two sets ☐
Ultimate Breathing Workout ☐
Bullfrogs- 40 reps ☐
Tongue Pushups- 40 reps ☐

EVENING ROUTINE

60-90 minutes before bedtime

Ultimate Isolation Exercise (Dynamically loud on YAY) ☐
Cardio singing- Sing four songs on lip bubbles ☐
Voice & Body Cool Down ☐

DAY 2

MORNING ROUTINE

Start time between 5:00 AM-7:00 AM

Tabata Breathing ☐
Mind/Body Process ☐
16-ounce water mixture (SVH + DMG) ☐
Five Rites- Eight reps each ☐
VSR/VSP/Voice RX Warm up ☐

Sirens 1-5-1
YAH + bodyweight routine ☐
YAY + bodyweight routine ☐
YEE + bodyweight routine ☐
YOH + bodyweight routine ☐
YOU + bodyweight routine ☐
YAH-AY-AH + bodyweight routine ☐
YAY-EE-AY + bodyweight routine ☐
YEE-OH-EE + bodyweight routine ☐
YOH-OU-OH + bodyweight routine ☐
YOU-AH-OU + bodyweight routine ☐
Voice & Body Cool Down ☐

Voice Juice ☐

DAY 2

AFTERNOON ROUTINE

Start time between 12:00PM-5:00PM

Total Body Cardio- Two sets ☐
Ultimate Breathing Workout ☐
Platysma Pull ups- 20 reps ☐
Head Curls- 20 reps front and back ☐

EVENING ROUTINE

60-90 minutes before bedtime

Ultimate Isolation Exercise (Dynamically loud on YEE) ☐
Cardio singing- Sing four songs while humming (mmm) ☐
Voice & Body Cool Down ☐

DAY 3

MORNING ROUTINE

Start time between 5:00 AM-7:00 AM

Tabata Breathing ☐
Mind/Body Process ☐
16-ounce water mixture (SVH + DMG) ☐
Five Rites- Nine reps each ☐
VSR/VSP/Voice RX Warm up ☐

Sirens 1-5-1
YAH + bodyweight routine ☐
YAY + bodyweight routine ☐
YEE + bodyweight routine ☐
YOH + bodyweight routine ☐
YOU + bodyweight routine ☐
YAH-AY-AH + bodyweight routine ☐
YAY-EE-AY + bodyweight routine ☐
YEE-OH-EE + bodyweight routine ☐
YOH-OU-OH + bodyweight routine ☐
YOU-AH-OU + bodyweight routine ☐
Voice & Body Cool Down ☐

Voice Juice ☐

DAY 3

AFTERNOON ROUTINE

Start time between 12:00PM-5:00PM

Total Body Cardio- Two sets ☐
Ultimate Breathing Workout ☐
Bullfrogs- 40 reps ☐
Tongue Pushups- 40 reps ☐

EVENING ROUTINE

60-90 minutes before bedtime

Ultimate Isolation Exercise (Dynamically loud on YOH) ☐
Cardio singing- Sing four songs at low volume ☐
Voice & Body Cool Down ☐

DAY 4

MORNING ROUTINE

Start time between 5:00 AM-7:00 AM

Tabata Breathing   ☐
Mind/Body Process   ☐
16-ounce water mixture (SVH + DMG)   ☐
Five Rites- Ten reps each   ☐
VSR/VSP/Voice RX Warm up   ☐

Sirens 1-5-1
YAH + bodyweight routine   ☐
YAY + bodyweight routine   ☐
YEE + bodyweight routine   ☐
YOH + bodyweight routine   ☐
YOU + bodyweight routine   ☐
YAH-AY-AH + bodyweight routine   ☐
YAY-EE-AY + bodyweight routine   ☐
YEE-OH-EE + bodyweight routine   ☐
YOH-OU-OH + bodyweight routine   ☐
YOU-AH-OU + bodyweight routine   ☐
Voice & Body Cool Down   ☐

Voice Juice   ☐

DAY 4

AFTERNOON ROUTINE

Start time between 12:00PM-5:00PM

Total Body Cardio- Two sets ☐
Ultimate Breathing Workout ☐
Platysma Pull ups- 20 reps ☐
Head Curls- 20 reps front and back ☐

EVENING ROUTINE

60-90 minutes before bedtime

Ultimate Isolation Exercise (Dynamically loud on YOU) ☐
Cardio singing- Sing four songs at medium volume ☐
Voice & Body Cool Down ☐

DAY 5

MORNING ROUTINE

Start time between 5:00 AM-7:00 AM

Tabata Breathing ☐
Mind/Body Process ☐
16-ounce water mixture (SVH + DMG) ☐
Five Rites- Eleven reps each ☐
VSR/VSP/Voice RX Warm up ☐

Sirens 1-5-1
YAH + bodyweight routine ☐
YAY + bodyweight routine ☐
YEE + bodyweight routine ☐
YOH + bodyweight routine ☐
YOU + bodyweight routine ☐
YAH-AY-AH + bodyweight routine ☐
YAY-EE-AY + bodyweight routine ☐
YEE-OH-EE + bodyweight routine ☐
YOH-OU-OH + bodyweight routine ☐
YOU-AH-OU + bodyweight routine ☐
Voice & Body Cool Down ☐

Voice Juice ☐

DAY 5

AFTERNOON ROUTINE

Start time between 12:00PM-5:00PM

Total Body Cardio- Two sets ☐
Ultimate Breathing Workout ☐
Bullfrogs- 40 reps ☐
Tongue Pushups- 40 reps ☐

EVENING ROUTINE

60-90 minutes before bedtime

Ultimate Isolation Exercise (Dynamically soft on YAH) ☐
Cardio singing- Sing four songs at full volume ☐
Voice & Body Cool Down ☐

DAY 6

MORNING ROUTINE

Start time between 5:00 AM-7:00 AM

Tabata Breathing	☐
Mind/Body Process	☐
16-ounce water mixture (SVH + DMG)	☐
Five Rites- Twelve reps each	☐
VSR/VSP/Voice RX Warm up	☐

Sirens 1-5-1

YAH + bodyweight routine	☐
YAY + bodyweight routine	☐
YEE + bodyweight routine	☐
YOH + bodyweight routine	☐
YOU + bodyweight routine	☐
YAH-AY-AH + bodyweight routine	☐
YAY-EE-AY + bodyweight routine	☐
YEE-OH-EE + bodyweight routine	☐
YOH-OU-OH + bodyweight routine	☐
YOU-AH-OU + bodyweight routine	☐
Voice & Body Cool Down	☐

Voice Juice	☐

DAY 6

AFTERNOON ROUTINE

Start time between 12:00PM-5:00PM

Total Body Cardio- Two sets ☐
Ultimate Breathing Workout ☐
Platysma Pull ups- 20 reps ☐
Head Curls- 20 reps front and back ☐

EVENING ROUTINE

60-90 minutes before bedtime

Ultimate Isolation Exercise (Dynamically soft on YAY) ☐
Cardio singing- Sing four songs at full volume ☐
Voice & Body Cool Down ☐

REST DAY

Congratulations, you've made it through Week 2. Take today to reflect on how you are beginning to adapt to this program. It is becoming a way of life for you, and though we've progressed, increasing reps and changing the vocal exercises, it may feel as if it was easier the second week than the first. You are starting to condition your body for a strenuous workout by building muscle.

As usual, don't forget to warm up in the shower with VSR/VSP while singing along to *Voice RX.* The shower routine is my warm-up routine whenever I am on a rest day, on tour, or whenever I am not working through V30.

In addition, today is your second juice fast day. Sorry about your luck. See you tomorrow.

WEEK 3

During the third week we'll increase our reps to 60% of total reps of the bodyweight routine. This week, you should start to feel the burn. Each set now consists of the following:

Push-ups: 6 reps
Chin-ups: 3 reps
Triceps dips: 6 reps
Sit-ups into leg lifts: 6 reps
Squats: 12 reps
Torso twists: 6 reps
Jump rope: 30 reps

Remember, 6-3-6-6-12-6-30. This week, Sirens combine thirds and fifths. Vowel modifications will also change. It's also time to move our pitch up three more steps. Males with a break at E4 are now working up to G#4 as opposed to F4 from last week. Females with a break point of A4 will now work up to C#5 instead of A#4 from last week. Last week we only moved up two notes, but now the work is getting intense. We must proceed at this rate to strengthen the mid-range and work it seamlessly into the high range by Week 5. Males would start at G#2-C3-G#2-D#3-G#2 (or 1-3-1-5-1), working up to C#4-F4-C#4-G#4-C4. Females would start at C#3-F3-C#3-G#3-C3, working up to F#4-A#4-F#4-C#5-F#4. If your break doesn't occur at E4 (males) or A4 (females), adjust the pitch accordingly. Remember, if the low notes are too low, adjust your scale accordingly at the bottom, but always aim for the correct note on the top of the scale.

DAY 1

MORNING ROUTINE

Start time between 5:00 AM-7:00 AM

Tabata Breathing ☐
Mind/Body Process ☐
16-ounce water mixture (SVH + DMG) ☐
Five Rites- Thirteen reps each ☐
VSR/VSP/Voice RX Warm up ☐

Sirens 1-3-1-5-1
YAH + bodyweight routine ☐
YAY + bodyweight routine ☐
YEE + bodyweight routine ☐
YOH + bodyweight routine ☐
YOU + bodyweight routine ☐
YAH-AY-EE-OH-OU + bodyweight routine ☐
YAY-EE-OH-OU-AH + bodyweight routine ☐
YEE-OH-OU-AH-AY + bodyweight routine ☐
YOH-OU-AH-AY-EE + bodyweight routine ☐
YOU-AH-AY-EE-OH + bodyweight routine ☐
Voice & Body Cool Down ☐

Voice Juice ☐

DAY 1

AFTERNOON ROUTINE

Start time between 12:00PM-5:00PM

Total Body Cardio- Three sets ☐
Ultimate Breathing Workout ☐
Bullfrogs- 60 reps ☐
Tongue Pushups- 60 reps ☐

EVENING ROUTINE

60-90 minutes before bedtime

Ultimate Isolation Exercise (Dynamically soft on YEE) ☐
Cardio singing- Sing six songs on lip bubbles ☐
Voice & Body Cool Down ☐

DAY 2

MORNING ROUTINE

Start time between 5:00 AM-7:00 AM

Tabata Breathing ☐
Mind/Body Process ☐
16-ounce water mixture (SVH + DMG) ☐
Five Rites- Fourteen reps each ☐
VSR/VSP/Voice RX Warm up ☐

Sirens 1-3-1-5-1
YAH + bodyweight routine ☐
YAY + bodyweight routine ☐
YEE + bodyweight routine ☐
YOH + bodyweight routine ☐
YOU + bodyweight routine ☐
YAH-AY-EE-OH-OU + bodyweight routine ☐
YAY-EE-OH-OU-AH + bodyweight routine ☐
YEE-OH-OU-AH-AY + bodyweight routine ☐
YOH-OU-AH-AY-EE + bodyweight routine ☐
YOU-AH-AY-EE-OH + bodyweight routine ☐
Voice & Body Cool Down ☐

Voice Juice ☐

DAY 2

AFTERNOON ROUTINE

Start time between 12:00PM-5:00PM

Total Body Cardio- Three sets ☐
Ultimate Breathing Workout ☐
Platysma Pull ups- 30 reps ☐
Head Curls- 30 reps front and back ☐

EVENING ROUTINE

60-90 minutes before bedtime

Ultimate Isolation Exercise (Dynamically soft on YOH) ☐
Cardio singing- Sing six songs while humming (mmm) ☐
Voice & Body Cool Down ☐

DAY 3

MORNING ROUTINE

Start time between 5:00 AM-7:00 AM

Tabata Breathing ☐
Mind/Body Process ☐
16-ounce water mixture (SVH + DMG) ☐
Five Rites- Fifteen reps each ☐
VSR/VSP/Voice RX Warm up ☐

Sirens 1-3-1-5-1
YAH + bodyweight routine ☐
YAY + bodyweight routine ☐
YEE + bodyweight routine ☐
YOH + bodyweight routine ☐
YOU + bodyweight routine ☐
YAH-AY-EE-OH-OU + bodyweight routine ☐
YAY-EE-OH-OU-AH + bodyweight routine ☐
YEE-OH-OU-AH-AY + bodyweight routine ☐
YOH-OU-AH-AY-EE + bodyweight routine ☐
YOU-AH-AY-EE-OH + bodyweight routine ☐
Voice & Body Cool Down ☐

Voice Juice ☐

DAY 3

AFTERNOON ROUTINE

Start time between 12:00PM-5:00PM

Total Body Cardio- Three sets ☐
Ultimate Breathing Workout ☐
Bullfrogs- 60 reps ☐
Tongue Pushups- 60 reps ☐

EVENING ROUTINE

60-90 minutes before bedtime

Ultimate Isolation Exercise (Dynamically soft on YOU) ☐
Cardio singing- Sing six songs at low volume ☐
Voice & Body Cool Down ☐

DAY 4

MORNING ROUTINE

Start time between 5:00 AM-7:00 AM

Tabata Breathing ☐
Mind/Body Process ☐
16-ounce water mixture (SVH + DMG) ☐
Five Rites- Sixteen reps each ☐
VSR/VSP/Voice RX Warm up ☐

Sirens 1-3-1-5-1
YAH + bodyweight routine ☐
YAY + bodyweight routine ☐
YEE + bodyweight routine ☐
YOH + bodyweight routine ☐
YOU + bodyweight routine ☐
YAH-AY-EE-OH-OU + bodyweight routine ☐
YAY-EE-OH-OU-AH + bodyweight routine ☐
YEE-OH-OU-AH-AY + bodyweight routine ☐
YOH-OU-AH-AY-EE + bodyweight routine ☐
YOU-AH-AY-EE-OH + bodyweight routine ☐
Voice & Body Cool Down ☐

Voice Juice ☐

DAY 4

AFTERNOON ROUTINE

Start time between 12:00PM-5:00PM

Total Body Cardio- Three sets ☐
Ultimate Breathing Workout ☐
Platysma Pull ups- 30 reps ☐
Head Curls- 30 reps front and back ☐

EVENING ROUTINE

60-90 minutes before bedtime

Ultimate Isolation Exercise (Dynamically loud on YAH) ☐
Cardio singing- Sing six songs at medium volume ☐
Voice & Body Cool Down ☐

DAY 5

MORNING ROUTINE

Start time between 5:00 AM-7:00 AM

Tabata Breathing ☐
Mind/Body Process ☐
16-ounce water mixture (SVH + DMG) ☐
Five Rites- Seventeen reps each ☐
VSR/VSP/Voice RX Warm up ☐

Sirens 1-3-1-5-1
YAH + bodyweight routine ☐
YAY + bodyweight routine ☐
YEE + bodyweight routine ☐
YOH + bodyweight routine ☐
YOU + bodyweight routine ☐
YAH-AY-EE-OH-OU + bodyweight routine ☐
YAY-EE-OH-OU-AH + bodyweight routine ☐
YEE-OH-OU-AH-AY + bodyweight routine ☐
YOH-OU-AH-AY-EE + bodyweight routine ☐
YOU-AH-AY-EE-OH + bodyweight routine ☐
Voice & Body Cool Down ☐

Voice Juice ☐

DAY 5

AFTERNOON ROUTINE

Start time between 12:00PM-5:00PM

Total Body Cardio- Three sets ☐
Ultimate Breathing Workout ☐
Bullfrogs- 60 reps ☐
Tongue Pushups- 60 reps ☐

EVENING ROUTINE

60-90 minutes before bedtime

Ultimate Isolation Exercise (Dynamically loud on YAY) ☐
Cardio singing- Sing six songs at full volume ☐
Voice & Body Cool Down ☐

DAY 6

MORNING ROUTINE

Start time between 5:00 AM-7:00 AM

Tabata Breathing ☐
Mind/Body Process ☐
16-ounce water mixture (SVH + DMG) ☐
Five Rites- Eighteen reps each ☐
VSR/VSP/Voice RX Warm up ☐

Sirens 1-3-1-5-1
YAH + bodyweight routine ☐
YAY + bodyweight routine ☐
YEE + bodyweight routine ☐
YOH + bodyweight routine ☐
YOU + bodyweight routine ☐
YAH-AY-EE-OH-OU + bodyweight routine ☐
YAY-EE-OH-OU-AH + bodyweight routine ☐
YEE-OH-OU-AH-AY + bodyweight routine ☐
YOH-OU-AH-AY-EE + bodyweight routine ☐
YOU-AH-AY-EE-OH + bodyweight routine ☐
Voice & Body Cool Down ☐

Voice Juice ☐

DAY 6

AFTERNOON ROUTINE

Start time between 12:00PM-5:00PM

Total Body Cardio- Three sets ☐
Ultimate Breathing Workout ☐
Platysma Pull ups- 30 reps ☐
Head Curls- 30 reps front and back ☐

EVENING ROUTINE

60-90 minutes before bedtime

Ultimate Isolation Exercise (Dynamically loud on YEE) ☐
Cardio singing- Sing six songs at full volume ☐
Voice & Body Cool Down ☐

REST DAY

You're now past the halfway mark. How does it feel? Take this rest day to view your voice and body. Look at yourself in the mirror. Do you look leaner? Adding a little definition? Record yourself singing. How does your voice feel? Do you feel stronger, can you sing higher or lower, do you sound better? I'm sure you've answered YES to these questions, but even if you said NO, don't worry, building muscle and building the voice does take time.

Since Week 3 is finished, you are over the vocal boot camp hump, which means you've finished the easy part. The next two weeks are going to be brutal. So, take your day of rest (but don't forget to warm up), and, as a treat, I won't ask you to juice today. Go out and enjoy a nice meal with friends and family. Spoil yourself today, because tomorrow you WILL be crying!

WEEK 4

During the fourth week we'll increase our reps to 80% of total reps per bodyweight routine. You may have to pick up the pace as you flow through the bodyweight routine in order to attempt to complete each set before each Siren set is finished. Again, if you finish one before the other (Sirens or bodyweight exercises), that's perfectly acceptable; just be sure to complete all requirements per set. Each set now consists of the following:

Push-ups: 8 reps
Chin-ups: 4 reps
Triceps dips: 8 reps
Sit-ups into leg lifts: 8 reps
Squats: 16 reps
Torso twists: 8 reps
Jump rope: 40 reps

Remember, 8-4-8-8-16-8-40. This week, Sirens combine thirds, fifths, and octaves. It's also time to raise our pitch by three half steps. Males with a typical break at E4 will be working up to B4, as opposed to G#4 from last week. Females with a typical break point of A4 will now work up to E5 instead of C#5 from last week. This week is a bit different, as we change our point of reference on the fifth. Males with a typical break point at D#4 would play a scale as G#2-C3-G#2-D#3-G#2-G#3-G#2 (or 1-3-1-5-1-8-1), working to B3-D#4-B3-F#4-B3-B4-B3. Females would start at C#3-E3-C#3-G#3-C#3-C#4-C#3, working up to E4-G#4-E4-B4-E4-E5-E4. If your break doesn't occur at E4 (males) or A4 (females), adjust the top note up or down accordingly. As usual, you can adjust the bottom starting point, if needed.

DAY 1

MORNING ROUTINE

Start time between 5:00 AM-7:00 AM

Tabata Breathing □
16-ounce water mixture (SVH + DMG) □
One dropperful each of Sinus Clear Out + DMG □
Five Rites- Nineteen reps each □
VSR/VSP/Voice RX Warm up □

Sirens 1-3-1-5-1-8-1
YAH + bodyweight routine □
YAY + bodyweight routine □
YEE + bodyweight routine □
YOH + bodyweight routine □
YOU + bodyweight routine □
YAH-AY-EE-OH-OU-AH-AY + bodyweight routine □
YAY-EE-OH-OU-AH-AY-EE + bodyweight routine □
YEE-OH-OU-AH-AY-EE-OH + bodyweight routine □
YOH-OU-AH-AY-EE-OH-OU + bodyweight routine □
YOU-AH-AY-EE-OH-OU-AH + bodyweight routine □
Voice & Body Cool Down □

Voice Juice □

DAY 1

AFTERNOON ROUTINE

Start time between 12:00PM-5:00PM

Total Body Cardio- Four sets ☐
Ultimate Breathing Workout ☐
Bullfrogs- 80 reps ☐
Tongue Pushups- 80 reps ☐

EVENING ROUTINE

60-90 minutes before bedtime

Ultimate Isolation Exercise (Dynamically loud on YOH) ☐
Cardio singing- Sing eight songs on lip bubbles ☐
Voice & Body Cool Down ☐

DAY 2

MORNING ROUTINE

Start time between 5:00 AM-7:00 AM

Tabata Breathing ☐
Mind/Body Process ☐
16-ounce water mixture (SVH + DMG) ☐
Five Rites- Twenty reps each ☐
VSR/VSP/Voice RX Warm up ☐

Sirens 1-3-1-5-1-8-1
YAH + bodyweight routine ☐
YAY + bodyweight routine ☐
YEE + bodyweight routine ☐
YOH + bodyweight routine ☐
YOU + bodyweight routine ☐
YAH-AY-EE-OH-OU-AH-AY + bodyweight routine ☐
YAY-EE-OH-OU-AH-AY-EE + bodyweight routine ☐
YEE-OH-OU-AH-AY-EE-OH + bodyweight routine ☐
YOH-OU-AH-AY-EE-OH-OU + bodyweight routine ☐
YOU-AH-AY-EE-OH-OU-AH + bodyweight routine ☐
Voice & Body Cool Down ☐

Voice Juice ☐

DAY 2

AFTERNOON ROUTINE

Start time between 12:00PM-5:00PM

Total Body Cardio- Four sets ☐
Ultimate Breathing Workout ☐
Platysma Pull ups- 40 reps ☐
Head Curls- 40 reps front and back ☐

EVENING ROUTINE

60-90 minutes before bedtime

Ultimate Isolation Exercise (Dynamically loud on YOU) ☐
Cardio singing- Sing eight songs while humming (mmm) ☐
Voice & Body Cool Down ☐

DAY 3

MORNING ROUTINE

Start time between 5:00 AM-7:00 AM

Tabata Breathing ☐
Mind/Body Process ☐
16-ounce water mixture (SVH + DMG) ☐
Five Rites- Twenty-one reps each ☐
VSR/VSP/Voice RX Warm up ☐

Sirens 1-3-1-5-1-8-1
YAH + bodyweight routine ☐
YAY + bodyweight routine ☐
YEE + bodyweight routine ☐
YOH + bodyweight routine ☐
YOU + bodyweight routine ☐
YAH-AY-EE-OH-OU-AH-AY + bodyweight routine ☐
YAY-EE-OH-OU-AH-AY-EE + bodyweight routine ☐
YEE-OH-OU-AH-AY-EE-OH + bodyweight routine ☐
YOH-OU-AH-AY-EE-OH-OU + bodyweight routine ☐
YOU-AH-AY-EE-OH-OU-AH + bodyweight routine ☐
Voice & Body Cool Down ☐

Voice Juice ☐

DAY 3

AFTERNOON ROUTINE

Start time between 12:00PM-5:00PM

Total Body Cardio- Four sets ☐
Ultimate Breathing Workout ☐
Bullfrogs- 80 reps ☐
Tongue Pushups- 80 reps ☐

EVENING ROUTINE

60-90 minutes before bedtime

Ultimate Isolation Exercise (Dynamically soft on YAH) ☐
Cardio singing- Sing eight songs at low volume ☐
Voice & Body Cool Down ☐

DAY 4

MORNING ROUTINE

Start time between 5:00 AM-7:00 AM

Tabata Breathing   ☐
Mind/Body Process   ☐
16-ounce water mixture (SVH + DMG)   ☐
Five Rites- Twenty-one reps each   ☐
VSR/VSP/Voice RX Warm up   ☐

Sirens 1-3-1-5-1-8-1
YAH + bodyweight routine   ☐
YAY + bodyweight routine   ☐
YEE + bodyweight routine   ☐
YOH + bodyweight routine   ☐
YOU + bodyweight routine   ☐
YAH-AY-EE-OH-OU-AH-AY + bodyweight routine   ☐
YAY-EE-OH-OU-AH-AY-EE + bodyweight routine   ☐
YEE-OH-OU-AH-AY-EE-OH + bodyweight routine   ☐
YOH-OU-AH-AY-EE-OH-OU + bodyweight routine   ☐
YOU-AH-AY-EE-OH-OU-AH + bodyweight routine   ☐
Voice & Body Cool Down   ☐

Voice Juice   ☐

DAY 4

AFTERNOON ROUTINE

Start time between 12:00PM-5:00PM

Total Body Cardio- Four sets ☐
Ultimate Breathing Workout ☐
Platysma Pull ups- 40 reps ☐
Head Curls- 40 reps front and back ☐

EVENING ROUTINE

60-90 minutes before bedtime

Ultimate Isolation Exercise (Dynamically soft on YAY) ☐
Cardio singing- Sing eight songs at medium volume ☐
Voice & Body Cool Down ☐

DAY 5

MORNING ROUTINE

Start time between 5:00 AM-7:00 AM

Tabata Breathing   ☐
Mind/Body Process   ☐
16-ounce water mixture (SVH + DMG)   ☐
Five Rites- Twenty-one reps each   ☐
VSR/VSP/Voice RX Warm up   ☐

Sirens 1-3-1-5-1-8-1
YAH + bodyweight routine   ☐
YAY + bodyweight routine   ☐
YEE + bodyweight routine   ☐
YOH + bodyweight routine   ☐
YOU + bodyweight routine   ☐
YAH-AY-EE-OH-OU-AH-AY + bodyweight routine   ☐
YAY-EE-OH-OU-AH-AY-EE + bodyweight routine   ☐
YEE-OH-OU-AH-AY-EE-OH + bodyweight routine   ☐
YOH-OU-AH-AY-EE-OH-OU + bodyweight routine   ☐
YOU-AH-AY-EE-OH-OU-AH + bodyweight routine   ☐
Voice & Body Cool Down   ☐

Voice Juice   ☐

DAY 5

AFTERNOON ROUTINE

Start time between 12:00PM-5:00PM

Total Body Cardio- Four sets ☐
Ultimate Breathing Workout ☐
Bullfrogs- 80 reps ☐
Tongue Pushups- 80 reps ☐

EVENING ROUTINE

60-90 minutes before bedtime

Ultimate Isolation Exercise (Dynamically soft on YEE) ☐
Cardio singing- Sing eight songs at full volume ☐
Voice & Body Cool Down ☐

DAY 6

MORNING ROUTINE

Start time between 5:00 AM-7:00 AM

Tabata Breathing ☐
Mind/Body Process ☐
16-ounce water mixture (SVH + DMG) ☐
Five Rites- Twenty-one reps each ☐
VSR/VSP/Voice RX Warm up ☐

Sirens 1-3-1-5-1-8-1
YAH + bodyweight routine ☐
YAY + bodyweight routine ☐
YEE + bodyweight routine ☐
YOH + bodyweight routine ☐
YOU + bodyweight routine ☐
YAH-AY-EE-OH-OU-AH-AY + bodyweight routine ☐
YAY-EE-OH-OU-AH-AY-EE + bodyweight routine ☐
YEE-OH-OU-AH-AY-EE-OH + bodyweight routine ☐
YOH-OU-AH-AY-EE-OH-OU + bodyweight routine ☐
YOU-AH-AY-EE-OH-OU-AH + bodyweight routine ☐
Voice & Body Cool Down ☐

Voice Juice ☐

DAY 6

AFTERNOON ROUTINE

Start time between 12:00PM-5:00PM

Total Body Cardio- Four sets ☐
Ultimate Breathing Workout ☐
Platysma Pull ups- 40 reps ☐
Head Curls- 40 reps front and back ☐

EVENING ROUTINE

60-90 minutes before bedtime

Ultimate Isolation Exercise (Dynamically soft on YOH) ☐
Cardio singing- Sing eight songs at full volume ☐
Voice & Body Cool Down ☐

REST DAY

I bet you're thrilled to have another day off! How was it? As brutal as I promised? It gets easier. But first it gets harder, because next week is full throttle!

Warm up in the shower with VSR/VSP/*Voice RX*. We're back to juice fasting, too! Relax, drink up, maybe go jam on some tunes with friends, and I will see you tomorrow.

WEEK 5

During the final week you will be at 100% reps per set of the bodyweight routine. Last week you found your flow, now you must flow faster! Each set now consists of the following:

Push-ups: 10 reps
Chin-ups: 5 reps
Triceps dips: 10 reps
Sit-ups into leg lifts: 10 reps
Squats: 20 reps
Torso twists: 10 reps
Jump rope: 50 reps

Remember, 10-5-10-10-20-10-50. This final week, Sirens will test your breathing skills. It's time again to move our pitch up three more steps. Males with a typical break at E4 will be working up to D5, as opposed to B4 from last week. Females with a typical break point of A4 will now work up to G5 instead of E5 from last week.

"But, Jaime, I thought we were just working on the mid-range?" True, but I needed to get you above the second break. We all have a tendency to have another gear change in our voices, and reaching D5/G5 will typically place us above that second gear change to assure that we've covered the entire mid-range. Males would start at G#2-C3-G#2-D#3-G#2-G#3-G#2-D#3-G#2-C3-G#2 (or 1-3-1-5-1-8-1-5-1-3-1), working up to D4-F#4-D4-A4-D4-D5-D4-A4-D4-F#4-D4. Females would start at C#3-E3-C#3-G#3-C#3-C#4-C#3-G#3-C#3-E3-C#3, working up to G4-B4-G4-D4-G4-G5-G4-D4-G4-B4-G4. If your break doesn't occur at E4 (males) or A4 (females), adjust accordingly. In addition, adjust the bottom note, if needed. However, the lower you can train your voice, the better the foundation you will have to support a stronger mid-range. So try for the lower notes. Here we go, time for vocal boot camp hard-core style!

DAY 1

MORNING ROUTINE

Start time between 5:00 AM-7:00 AM

Tabata Breathing ☐
Mind/Body Process ☐
16-ounce water mixture (SVH + DMG) ☐
Five Rites- Twenty-one reps each ☐
VSR/VSP/Voice RX Warm up ☐

Sirens 1-3-1-5-1-8-1-5-1-3-1
YAH + bodyweight routine ☐
YAY + bodyweight routine ☐
YEE + bodyweight routine ☐
YOH + bodyweight routine ☐
YOU + bodyweight routine ☐
YAH-AY-EE-OH-OU-AH-AY-EE-OH-OU-AH + bw routine ☐
YAY-EE-OH-OU-AH-AY-EE-OH-OU-AH-AY + bw routine ☐
YEE-OH-OU-AH-AY-EE-OH-OU-AH-AY-EE + bw routine ☐
YOH-OU-AH-AY-EE-OH-OU-AH-AY-EE-OH + bw routine ☐
YOU-AH-AY-EE-OH-OU-AH-AY-EE-OH-OU + bw routine ☐
Voice & Body Cool Down ☐

Voice Juice ☐

DAY 1

AFTERNOON ROUTINE

Start time between 12:00PM-5:00PM

Total Body Cardio- Five sets ☐
Ultimate Breathing Workout ☐
Bullfrogs- 100 reps ☐
Tongue Pushups- 100 reps ☐

EVENING ROUTINE

60-90 minutes before bedtime

Ultimate Isolation Exercise (Dynamically soft on YOU) ☐
Cardio singing- Sing ten songs on lip bubbles ☐
Voice & Body Cool Down ☐

DAY 2

MORNING ROUTINE

Start time between 5:00 AM-7:00 AM

Tabata Breathing ☐
Mind/Body Process ☐
16-ounce water mixture (SVH + DMG) ☐
Five Rites- Twenty-one reps each ☐
VSR/VSP/Voice RX Warm up ☐

Sirens 1-3-1-5-1-8-1-5-1-3-1
YAH + bodyweight routine ☐
YAY + bodyweight routine ☐
YEE + bodyweight routine ☐
YOH + bodyweight routine ☐
YOU + bodyweight routine ☐
YAH-AY-EE-OH-OU-AH-AY-EE-OH-OU-AH + bw routine ☐
YAY-EE-OH-OU-AH-AY-EE-OH-OU-AH-AY + bw routine ☐
YEE-OH-OU-AH-AY-EE-OH-OU-AH-AY-EE + bw routine ☐
YOH-OU-AH-AY-EE-OH-OU-AH-AY-EE-OH + bw routine ☐
YOU-AH-AY-EE-OH-OU-AH-AY-EE-OH-OU + bw routine ☐
Voice & Body Cool Down ☐

Voice Juice ☐

DAY 2

AFTERNOON ROUTINE

Start time between 12:00PM-5:00PM

Total Body Cardio- Five sets ☐
Ultimate Breathing Workout ☐
Platysma Pull ups- 50 reps ☐
Head Curls- 50 reps front and back ☐

EVENING ROUTINE

60-90 minutes before bedtime

Ultimate Isolation Exercise (Dynamically loud on YAH) ☐
Cardio singing- Sing ten songs while humming (mmm) ☐
Voice & Body Cool Down ☐

DAY 3

MORNING ROUTINE

Start time between 5:00 AM-7:00 AM

Tabata Breathing   ☐
Mind/Body Process   ☐
16-ounce water mixture (SVH + DMG)   ☐
Five Rites- Twenty-one reps each   ☐
VSR/VSP/Voice RX Warm up   ☐

Sirens 1-3-1-5-1-8-1-5-1-3-1
YAH + bodyweight routine   ☐
YAY + bodyweight routine   ☐
YEE + bodyweight routine   ☐
YOH + bodyweight routine   ☐
YOU + bodyweight routine   ☐
YAH-AY-EE-OH-OU-AH-AY-EE-OH-OU-AH + bw routine   ☐
YAY-EE-OH-OU-AH-AY-EE-OH-OU-AH-AY + bw routine   ☐
YEE-OH-OU-AH-AY-EE-OH-OU-AH-AY-EE + bw routine   ☐
YOH-OU-AH-AY-EE-OH-OU-AH-AY-EE-OH + bw routine   ☐
YOU-AH-AY-EE-OH-OU-AH-AY-EE-OH-OU + bw routine   ☐
Voice & Body Cool Down   ☐

Voice Juice   ☐

DAY 3

AFTERNOON ROUTINE

Start time between 12:00PM-5:00PM

Total Body Cardio- Five sets ☐
Ultimate Breathing Workout ☐
Bullfrogs- 100 reps ☐
Tongue Pushups- 100 reps ☐

EVENING ROUTINE

60-90 minutes before bedtime

Ultimate Isolation Exercise (Dynamically loud on YAY) ☐
Cardio singing- Sing ten songs at low volume ☐
Voice & Body Cool Down ☐

DAY 4

MORNING ROUTINE

Start time between 5:00 AM-7:00 AM

Tabata Breathing ☐
Mind/Body Process ☐
16-ounce water mixture (SVH + DMG) ☐
Five Rites- Twenty-one reps each ☐
VSR/VSP/Voice RX Warm up ☐

Sirens 1-3-1-5-1-8-1-5-1-3-1
YAH + bodyweight routine ☐
YAY + bodyweight routine ☐
YEE + bodyweight routine ☐
YOH + bodyweight routine ☐
YOU + bodyweight routine ☐
YAH-AY-EE-OH-OU-AH-AY-EE-OH-OU-AH + bw routine ☐
YAY-EE-OH-OU-AH-AY-EE-OH-OU-AH-AY + bw routine ☐
YEE-OH-OU-AH-AY-EE-OH-OU-AH-AY-EE + bw routine ☐
YOH-OU-AH-AY-EE-OH-OU-AH-AY-EE-OH + bw routine ☐
YOU-AH-AY-EE-OH-OU-AH-AY-EE-OH-OU + bw routine ☐
Voice & Body Cool Down ☐

Voice Juice ☐

DAY 4

AFTERNOON ROUTINE

Start time between 12:00PM-5:00PM

Total Body Cardio- Five sets ☐
Ultimate Breathing Workout ☐
Platysma Pull ups- 50 reps ☐
Head Curls- 50 reps front and back ☐

EVENING ROUTINE

60-90 minutes before bedtime

Ultimate Isolation Exercise (Dynamically loud on YEE) ☐
Cardio singing- Sing ten songs at medium volume ☐
Voice & Body Cool Down ☐

DAY 5

MORNING ROUTINE

Start time between 5:00 AM-7:00 AM

Tabata Breathing ☐
Mind/Body Process ☐
16-ounce water mixture (SVH + DMG) ☐
Five Rites- Twenty-one reps each ☐
VSR/VSP/Voice RX Warm up ☐

Sirens 1-3-1-5-1-8-1-5-1-3-1
YAH + bodyweight routine ☐
YAY + bodyweight routine ☐
YEE + bodyweight routine ☐
YOH + bodyweight routine ☐
YOU + bodyweight routine ☐
YAH-AY-EE-OH-OU-AH-AY-EE-OH-OU-AH + bw routine ☐
YAY-EE-OH-OU-AH-AY-EE-OH-OU-AH-AY + bw routine ☐
YEE-OH-OU-AH-AY-EE-OH-OU-AH-AY-EE + bw routine ☐
YOH-OU-AH-AY-EE-OH-OU-AH-AY-EE-OH + bw routine ☐
YOU-AH-AY-EE-OH-OU-AH-AY-EE-OH-OU + bw routine ☐
Voice & Body Cool Down ☐

Voice Juice ☐

DAY 5

AFTERNOON ROUTINE

Start time between 12:00PM-5:00PM

Total Body Cardio- Five sets ☐
Ultimate Breathing Workout ☐
Bullfrogs- 100 reps ☐
Tongue Pushups- 100 reps ☐

EVENING ROUTINE

60-90 minutes before bedtime

Ultimate Isolation Exercise (Dynamically loud on YOH) ☐
Cardio singing- Sing ten songs at full volume ☐
Voice & Body Cool Down ☐

DAY 6

MORNING ROUTINE

Start time between 5:00 AM-7:00 AM

Tabata Breathing ☐
Mind/Body Process ☐
16-ounce water mixture (SVH + DMG) ☐
Five Rites- Twenty-one reps each ☐
VSR/VSP/Voice RX Warm up ☐

Sirens 1-3-1-5-1-8-1-5-1-3-1
YAH + bodyweight routine ☐
YAY + bodyweight routine ☐
YEE + bodyweight routine ☐
YOH + bodyweight routine ☐
YOU + bodyweight routine ☐
YAH-AY-EE-OH-OU-AH-AY-EE-OH-OU-AH + bw routine ☐
YAY-EE-OH-OU-AH-AY-EE-OH-OU-AH-AY + bw routine ☐
YEE-OH-OU-AH-AY-EE-OH-OU-AH-AY-EE + bw routine ☐
YOH-OU-AH-AY-EE-OH-OU-AH-AY-EE-OH + bw routine ☐
YOU-AH-AY-EE-OH-OU-AH-AY-EE-OH-OU + bw routine ☐
Voice & Body Cool Down ☐

Voice Juice ☐

DAY 6

AFTERNOON ROUTINE

Start time between 12:00PM-5:00PM

Total Body Cardio- Five sets ☐
Ultimate Breathing Workout ☐
Platysma Pull ups- 50 reps ☐
Head Curls- 50 reps front and back ☐

EVENING ROUTINE

60-90 minutes before bedtime

Ultimate Isolation Exercise (Dynamically loud on YOU) ☐
Cardio singing- Sing ten songs at full volume ☐
Voice & Body Cool Down ☐

REST DAY

CONGRATULATIONS
YOU HAVE COMPLETED THE V30 BOOT CAMP!

That is V30 hard-core vocal training at its finest. How do you feel? How do you look? How are you singing? You are now on your way to becoming a great singer as well as looking the part. You've dedicated your life to mastering your instrument, your voice, which is part of your body. I can't wait to hear you!

What you do beyond this point is up to you. You can stick with Week 5 as your main routine and continue building your voice, shedding fat, and adding lean muscle. If you DO plan to add muscle, please note that you'll need to boost your protein intake. This is a subject for another book, one I'm not qualified to write, so please research this on your own. If you feel burned out, take a vocal vacation for the next week and start fresh the following week. If you've reached your goal and just need to maintain, you can switch the routine up. You may want to drop the afternoon routine or do it every other day or every other week. You can back off the exercises by performing the reps and exercise scales from any of the five weeks. Bottom line, you must continue to work out the voice and body to maintain what you've gained. The harder you work, the further you'll progress.

If you've become a hard-core vocal boot camp maniac and need more resistance, add weight belts to increase your bodyweight as you perform the exercises. Another option is to increase the reps by 20%.

You can also slip in some vocal scales, such as *Jim Gillette's Vocal Power* scales. Stick to a daily plan. If you want more guidance, contact me to book a lesson at jaimevendera.com. While you're there, join the Vendera Vocal Academy, where we'll work together to become better singers.

Wait, we're not finished. Since I'm such a caring coach, I've added two more V30 routines to keep you living the V30 lifestyle. For you V30 maniacs who dare to take the challenge, I've created V30 Extreme. I won't lie; it's brutal squared. Even I'm not this extreme. The goal in V30 Extreme to become so proficient at each exercise that you can do ALL reps per exercise in a row, which means you'd perform 100 pushups before moving on to 50 chin-ups, 100 dips, 100 sit-ups into leg lifts, 100 mike-stand twists, and 500 rope jumps. I've also created a maintenance V30 program, which I use.

Cardio singing will be at full volume from this point forward. You've trained enough to know vocal technique. Now it's time to sing full volume every day. So, do you SERIOUSLY want to do this? Okay, bring it on, woman, and flip to the next page.

V30 EXTREME

WEEK 1

Our goal over the next five weeks is to condition your body until you can complete all reps for one exercise of the bodyweight routine before moving on to the next exercise. Do not worry if you don't finish a set of the bodyweight routine by the end of one Siren set, because in V30 Extreme, one Siren set will not be enough to cover one set of the bodyweight routine.

V30 Extreme will use the same vocal exercises as Week 5 of the original V30 vocal boot camp, but we will up reps on certain exercises, so read your daily log carefully. During the first week of V30 Extreme, you will double the number of reps per each set of the bodyweight routine, which means there are now only five sets instead of ten. Do not rush. You are allotted two Siren sets per set of the bodyweight routine. Each set now consists of the following:

Push-ups: 20 reps
Chin-ups: 10 reps
Triceps dips: 20 reps
Sit-ups into leg lifts: 20 reps
Squats: 40 reps
Torso twists: 20 reps
Jump rope: 100 reps

Remember 20-10-20-20-40-20-100. Let the torture begin ...

DAY 1

MORNING ROUTINE

Start time between 5:00 AM-7:00 AM

Tabata Breathing ☐
Mind/Body Process ☐
16-ounce water mixture (SVH + DMG) ☐
Five Rites- Twenty-one reps each ☐
VSR/VSP/Voice RX Warm up ☐

Sirens 1-3-1-5-1-8-1-5-1-3-1
YAH ☐
YAY + complete bodyweight routine first set ☐
YEE ☐
YOH + complete bodyweight routine second set ☐
YOU ☐
YAH-AY-EE-OH-OU-AH-AY-EE-OH-OU-AH + third set ☐
YAY-EE-OH-OU-AH-AY-EE-OH-OU-AH-AY ☐
YEE-OH-OU-AH-AY-EE-OH-OU-AH-AY-EE + fourth set ☐
YOH-OU-AH-AY-EE-OH-OU-AH-AY-EE-OH ☐
YOU-AH-AY-EE-OH-OU-AH-AY-EE-OH-OU + fifth set ☐
Voice & Body Cool Down ☐

Voice Juice ☐

DAY 1

AFTERNOON ROUTINE

Start time between 12:00PM-5:00PM

Total Body Cardio- Six sets ☐
Ultimate Breathing Workout ☐
Bullfrogs- 100 reps ☐
Tongue Pushups- 100 reps ☐

EVENING ROUTINE

60-90 minutes before bedtime

Ultimate Isolation Exercise (Dynamically soft on YAH) ☐
Cardio singing- Sing twelve songs at full volume ☐
Voice & Body Cool Down ☐

DAY 2

MORNING ROUTINE

Start time between 5:00 AM-7:00 AM

Tabata Breathing ☐
Mind/Body Process ☐
16-ounce water mixture (SVH + DMG) ☐
Five Rites- Twenty-one reps each ☐
VSR/VSP/Voice RX Warm up ☐

Sirens 1-3-1-5-1-8-1-5-1-3-1
YAH ☐
YAY + complete bodyweight routine first set ☐
YEE ☐
YOH + complete bodyweight routine second set ☐
YOU ☐
YAH-AY-EE-OH-OU-AH-AY-EE-OH-OU-AH + third set ☐
YAY-EE-OH-OU-AH-AY-EE-OH-OU-AH-AY ☐
YEE-OH-OU-AH-AY-EE-OH-OU-AH-AY-EE + fourth set ☐
YOH-OU-AH-AY-EE-OH-OU-AH-AY-EE-OH ☐
YOU-AH-AY-EE-OH-OU-AH-AY-EE-OH-OU + fifth set ☐
Voice & Body Cool Down ☐

Voice Juice ☐

DAY 2

AFTERNOON ROUTINE

Start time between 12:00PM-5:00PM

Total Body Cardio- Six sets ☐
Ultimate Breathing Workout ☐
Platysma Pull ups- 60 reps ☐
Head Curls- 60 reps front and back ☐

EVENING ROUTINE

60-90 minutes before bedtime

Ultimate Isolation Exercise (Dynamically soft on YAY) ☐
Cardio singing- Sing twelve songs at full volume ☐
Voice & Body Cool Down ☐

DAY 3

MORNING ROUTINE

Start time between 5:00 AM-7:00 AM

Tabata Breathing	☐
Mind/Body Process	☐
16-ounce water mixture (SVH + DMG)	☐
Five Rites- Twenty-one reps each	☐
VSR/VSP/Voice RX Warm up	☐

Sirens 1-3-1-5-1-8-1-5-1-3-1

YAH	☐
YAY + complete bodyweight routine first set	☐
YEE	☐
YOH + complete bodyweight routine second set	☐
YOU	☐
YAH-AY-EE-OH-OU-AH-AY-EE-OH-OU-AH + third set	☐
YAY-EE-OH-OU-AH-AY-EE-OH-OU-AH-AY	☐
YEE-OH-OU-AH-AY-EE-OH-OU-AH-AY-EE + fourth set	☐
YOH-OU-AH-AY-EE-OH-OU-AH-AY-EE-OH	☐
YOU-AH-AY-EE-OH-OU-AH-AY-EE-OH-OU + fifth set	☐
Voice & Body Cool Down	☐

Voice Juice	☐

DAY 3

AFTERNOON ROUTINE

Start time between 12:00PM-5:00PM

Total Body Cardio- Six sets ☐
Ultimate Breathing Workout ☐
Bullfrogs- 100 reps ☐
Tongue Pushups- 100 reps ☐

EVENING ROUTINE

60-90 minutes before bedtime

Ultimate Isolation Exercise (Dynamically soft on YEE) ☐
Cardio singing- Sing twelve songs at full volume ☐
Voice & Body Cool Down ☐

DAY 4

MORNING ROUTINE

Start time between 5:00 AM-7:00 AM

Tabata Breathing	☐
Mind/Body Process	☐
16-ounce water mixture (SVH + DMG)	☐
Five Rites- Twenty-one reps each	☐
VSR/VSP/Voice RX Warm up	☐

Sirens 1-3-1-5-1-8-1-5-1-3-1

YAH	☐
YAY + complete bodyweight routine first set	☐
YEE	☐
YOH + complete bodyweight routine second set	☐
YOU	☐
YAH-AY-EE-OH-OU-AH-AY-EE-OH-OU-AH + third set	☐
YAY-EE-OH-OU-AH-AY-EE-OH-OU-AH-AY	☐
YEE-OH-OU-AH-AY-EE-OH-OU-AH-AY-EE + fourth set	☐
YOH-OU-AH-AY-EE-OH-OU-AH-AY-EE-OH	☐
YOU-AH-AY-EE-OH-OU-AH-AY-EE-OH-OU + fifth set	☐
Voice & Body Cool Down	☐

Voice Juice	☐

DAY 4

AFTERNOON ROUTINE

Start time between 12:00PM-5:00PM

Total Body Cardio- Six sets ☐
Ultimate Breathing Workout ☐
Platysma Pull ups- 60 reps ☐
Head Curls- 60 reps front and back ☐

EVENING ROUTINE

60-90 minutes before bedtime

Ultimate Isolation Exercise (Dynamically soft on YOH) ☐
Cardio singing- Sing twelve songs at full volume ☐
Voice & Body Cool Down ☐

DAY 5

MORNING ROUTINE

Start time between 5:00 AM-7:00 AM

Tabata Breathing ☐
Mind/Body Process ☐
16-ounce water mixture (SVH + DMG) ☐
Five Rites- Twenty-one reps each ☐
VSR/VSP/Voice RX Warm up ☐

Sirens 1-3-1-5-1-8-1-5-1-3-1
YAH ☐
YAY + complete bodyweight routine first set ☐
YEE ☐
YOH + complete bodyweight routine second set ☐
YOU ☐
YAH-AY-EE-OH-OU-AH-AY-EE-OH-OU-AH + third set ☐
YAY-EE-OH-OU-AH-AY-EE-OH-OU-AH-AY ☐
YEE-OH-OU-AH-AY-EE-OH-OU-AH-AY-EE + fourth set ☐
YOH-OU-AH-AY-EE-OH-OU-AH-AY-EE-OH ☐
YOU-AH-AY-EE-OH-OU-AH-AY-EE-OH-OU + fifth set ☐
Voice & Body Cool Down ☐

Voice Juice ☐

DAY 5

AFTERNOON ROUTINE

Start time between 12:00PM-5:00PM

Total Body Cardio- Six sets ☐
Ultimate Breathing Workout ☐
Bullfrogs- 100 reps ☐
Tongue Pushups- 100 reps ☐

EVENING ROUTINE

60-90 minutes before bedtime

Ultimate Isolation Exercise (Dynamically soft on YOU) ☐
Cardio singing- Sing twelve songs at full volume ☐
Voice & Body Cool Down ☐

DAY 6

MORNING ROUTINE

Start time between 5:00 AM-7:00 AM

Tabata Breathing ☐
Mind/Body Process ☐
16-ounce water mixture (SVH + DMG) ☐
Five Rites- Twenty-one reps each ☐
VSR/VSP/Voice RX Warm up ☐

Sirens 1-3-1-5-1-8-1-5-1-3-1
YAH ☐
YAY + complete bodyweight routine first set ☐
YEE ☐
YOH + complete bodyweight routine second set ☐
YOU ☐
YAH-AY-EE-OH-OU-AH-AY-EE-OH-OU-AH + third set ☐
YAY-EE-OH-OU-AH-AY-EE-OH-OU-AH-AY ☐
YEE-OH-OU-AH-AY-EE-OH-OU-AH-AY-EE + fourth set ☐
YOH-OU-AH-AY-EE-OH-OU-AH-AY-EE-OH ☐
YOU-AH-AY-EE-OH-OU-AH-AY-EE-OH-OU + fifth set ☐
Voice & Body Cool Down ☐

Voice Juice ☐

DAY 6

AFTERNOON ROUTINE

Start time between 12:00PM-5:00PM

Total Body Cardio- Six sets ☐
Ultimate Breathing Workout ☐
Platysma Pull ups- 60 reps ☐
Head Curls- 60 reps front and back ☐

EVENING ROUTINE

60-90 minutes before bedtime

Ultimate Isolation Exercise (Dynamically loud on YAH) ☐
Cardio singing- Sing twelve songs at full volume ☐
Voice & Body Cool Down ☐

REST DAY

Phew, what a week! Are your muscles crying yet? Good, *mwahahaha*, but the pain is just beginning. As usual, take a rest day, but don't forget to warm up, and yes, oh yes, it's time again for another juice fast! Take lots of naps, because you'll need all your energy tomorrow morning!

V30 EXTREME

WEEK 2

Week 2 gets, well, a little more extreme. Now we're entering the zone where it may take you up to three Siren sets to complete one set of the bodyweight routine. You now have three bodyweight sets to complete, with the third set shorter in reps. Each set now consists of the following:

Push-ups: 40/40/20 reps
Chin-ups: 20/20/10 reps
Triceps dips: 40/40/20 reps
Sit-ups into leg lifts: 40/40/20 reps
Squats: 80/80/40 reps
Torso twists: 40/40/20 reps
Jump rope: 200/200/100 reps

Remember 40-20-40-40-80-40-200 for two sets and 20-10-20-20-40-20-100 for the last set. If you finish the third set before finishing your exercises, you can either continue jumping rope at a slower pace or choose to rest while finishing the vocal exercises.

DAY 1

MORNING ROUTINE

Start time between 5:00 AM-7:00 AM

Tabata Breathing ☐
Mind/Body Process ☐
16-ounce water mixture (SVH + DMG) ☐
Five Rites- Twenty-one reps each ☐
VSR/VSP/Voice RX Warm up ☐

Sirens 1-3-1-5-1-8-1-5-1-3-1
YAH ☐
YAY ☐
YEE + complete bodyweight routine first set ☐
YOH ☐
YOU ☐
YAH-AY-EE-OH-OU-AH-AY-EE-OH-OU-AH + second set ☐
YAY-EE-OH-OU-AH-AY-EE-OH-OU-AH-AY ☐
YEE-OH-OU-AH-AY-EE-OH-OU-AH-AY-EE ☐
YOH-OU-AH-AY-EE-OH-OU-AH-AY-EE-OH + third set ☐
YOU-AH-AY-EE-OH-OU-AH-AY-EE-OH-OU + rest ☐
Voice & Body Cool Down ☐

Voice Juice ☐

DAY 1

AFTERNOON ROUTINE

Start time between 12:00PM-5:00PM

Total Body Cardio- Seven sets ☐
Ultimate Breathing Workout ☐
Bullfrogs- 200 reps ☐
Tongue Pushups- 200 reps ☐

EVENING ROUTINE

60-90 minutes before bedtime

Ultimate Isolation Exercise (Dynamically loud on YAY) ☐
Cardio singing- Sing fourteen songs at full volume ☐
Voice & Body Cool Down ☐

DAY 2

MORNING ROUTINE

Start time between 5:00 AM-7:00 AM

Tabata Breathing ☐
Mind/Body Process ☐
16-ounce water mixture (SVH + DMG) ☐
Five Rites- Twenty-one reps each ☐
VSR/VSP/Voice RX Warm up ☐

Sirens 1-3-1-5-1-8-1-5-1-3-1
YAH ☐
YAY ☐
YEE + complete bodyweight routine first set ☐
YOH ☐
YOU ☐
YAH-AY-EE-OH-OU-AH-AY-EE-OH-OU-AH + second set ☐
YAY-EE-OH-OU-AH-AY-EE-OH-OU-AH-AY ☐
YEE-OH-OU-AH-AY-EE-OH-OU-AH-AY-EE ☐
YOH-OU-AH-AY-EE-OH-OU-AH-AY-EE-OH + third set ☐
YOU-AH-AY-EE-OH-OU-AH-AY-EE-OH-OU + rest ☐
Voice & Body Cool Down ☐

Voice Juice ☐

DAY 2

AFTERNOON ROUTINE

Start time between 12:00PM-5:00PM

Total Body Cardio- Seven sets ☐
Ultimate Breathing Workout ☐
Platysma Pull ups- 70 reps ☐
Head Curls- 70 reps front and back ☐

EVENING ROUTINE

60-90 minutes before bedtime

Ultimate Isolation Exercise (Dynamically loud on YEE) ☐
Cardio singing- Sing fourteen songs at full volume ☐
Voice & Body Cool Down ☐

DAY 3

MORNING ROUTINE

Start time between 5:00 AM-7:00 AM

Tabata Breathing ☐

Mind/Body Process ☐

16-ounce water mixture (SVH + DMG) ☐

Five Rites- Twenty-one reps each ☐

VSR/VSP/Voice RX Warm up ☐

Sirens 1-3-1-5-1-8-1-5-1-3-1

YAH ☐

YAY ☐

YEE + complete bodyweight routine first set ☐

YOH ☐

YOU ☐

YAH-AY-EE-OH-OU-AH-AY-EE-OH-OU-AH + second set ☐

YAY-EE-OH-OU-AH-AY-EE-OH-OU-AH-AY ☐

YEE-OH-OU-AH-AY-EE-OH-OU-AH-AY-EE ☐

YOH-OU-AH-AY-EE-OH-OU-AH-AY-EE-OH + third set ☐

YOU-AH-AY-EE-OH-OU-AH-AY-EE-OH-OU + rest ☐

Voice & Body Cool Down ☐

Voice Juice ☐

DAY 3

AFTERNOON ROUTINE

Start time between 12:00PM-5:00PM

Total Body Cardio- Seven sets ☐
Ultimate Breathing Workout ☐
Bullfrogs- 200 reps ☐
Tongue Pushups- 200 reps ☐

EVENING ROUTINE

60-90 minutes before bedtime

Ultimate Isolation Exercise (Dynamically loud on YOH) ☐
Cardio singing- Sing fourteen songs at full volume ☐
Voice & Body Cool Down ☐

DAY 4

MORNING ROUTINE

Start time between 5:00 AM-7:00 AM

Tabata Breathing   ☐
Mind/Body Process   ☐
16-ounce water mixture (SVH + DMG)   ☐
Five Rites- Twenty-one reps each   ☐
VSR/VSP/Voice RX Warm up   ☐

Sirens 1-3-1-5-1-8-1-5-1-3-1
YAH   ☐
YAY   ☐
YEE + complete bodyweight routine first set   ☐
YOH   ☐
YOU   ☐
YAH-AY-EE-OH-OU-AH-AY-EE-OH-OU-AH + second set   ☐
YAY-EE-OH-OU-AH-AY-EE-OH-OU-AH-AY   ☐
YEE-OH-OU-AH-AY-EE-OH-OU-AH-AY-EE   ☐
YOH-OU-AH-AY-EE-OH-OU-AH-AY-EE-OH + third set   ☐
YOU-AH-AY-EE-OH-OU-AH-AY-EE-OH-OU + rest   ☐
Voice & Body Cool Down   ☐

Voice Juice   ☐

DAY 4

AFTERNOON ROUTINE

Start time between 12:00PM-5:00PM

Total Body Cardio- Seven sets ☐
Ultimate Breathing Workout ☐
Platysma Pull ups- 70 reps ☐
Head Curls- 70 reps front and back ☐

EVENING ROUTINE

60-90 minutes before bedtime

Ultimate Isolation Exercise (Dynamically loud on YOU) ☐
Cardio singing- Sing fourteen songs at full volume ☐
Voice & Body Cool Down ☐

DAY 5

MORNING ROUTINE

Start time between 5:00 AM-7:00 AM

Tabata Breathing ☐
Mind/Body Process ☐
16-ounce water mixture (SVH + DMG) ☐
Five Rites- Twenty-one reps each ☐
VSR/VSP/Voice RX Warm up ☐

Sirens 1-3-1-5-1-8-1-5-1-3-1
YAH ☐
YAY ☐
YEE + complete bodyweight routine first set ☐
YOH ☐
YOU ☐
YAH-AY-EE-OH-OU-AH-AY-EE-OH-OU-AH + second set ☐
YAY-EE-OH-OU-AH-AY-EE-OH-OU-AH-AY ☐
YEE-OH-OU-AH-AY-EE-OH-OU-AH-AY-EE ☐
YOH-OU-AH-AY-EE-OH-OU-AH-AY-EE-OH + third set ☐
YOU-AH-AY-EE-OH-OU-AH-AY-EE-OH-OU + rest ☐
Voice & Body Cool Down ☐

Voice Juice ☐

DAY 5

AFTERNOON ROUTINE

Start time between 12:00PM-5:00PM

Total Body Cardio- Seven sets   ☐
Ultimate Breathing Workout   ☐
Bullfrogs- 200 reps   ☐
Tongue Pushups- 200 reps   ☐

EVENING ROUTINE

60-90 minutes before bedtime

Ultimate Isolation Exercise (Dynamically soft on YAH)   ☐
Cardio singing- Sing fourteen songs at full volume   ☐
Voice & Body Cool Down   ☐

DAY 6

MORNING ROUTINE

Start time between 5:00 AM-7:00 AM

Tabata Breathing	☐
Mind/Body Process	☐
16-ounce water mixture (SVH + DMG)	☐
Five Rites- Twenty-one reps each	☐
VSR/VSP/Voice RX Warm up	☐

Sirens 1-3-1-5-1-8-1-5-1-3-1

YAH	☐
YAY	☐
YEE + complete bodyweight routine first set	☐
YOH	☐
YOU	☐
YAH-AY-EE-OH-OU-AH-AY-EE-OH-OU-AH + second set	☐
YAY-EE-OH-OU-AH-AY-EE-OH-OU-AH-AY	☐
YEE-OH-OU-AH-AY-EE-OH-OU-AH-AY-EE	☐
YOH-OU-AH-AY-EE-OH-OU-AH-AY-EE-OH + third set	☐
YOU-AH-AY-EE-OH-OU-AH-AY-EE-OH-OU + rest	☐
Voice & Body Cool Down	☐

Voice Juice	☐

DAY 6

AFTERNOON ROUTINE

Start time between 12:00PM-5:00PM

Total Body Cardio- Seven sets ☐
Ultimate Breathing Workout ☐
Platysma Pull ups- 70 reps ☐
Head Curls- 70 reps front and back ☐

EVENING ROUTINE

60-90 minutes before bedtime

Ultimate Isolation Exercise (Dynamically soft on YAY) ☐
Cardio singing- Sing fourteen songs at full volume ☐
Voice & Body Cool Down ☐

REST DAY

Rinse, repeat, it's time for a treat. Today you get to take another vocal break. Well, except for that pesky warm-up thing you have to do in the shower. It's also time to juice the good stuff. If you're tired of the juice combo I gave you, there are TONS of books available with juice recipes. Or search online for "juicing recipes" and you'll find countless combinations that'll make your mouth water. See you tomorrow.

V30 EXTREME

WEEK 3

Week 3 continues to increase the reps per each set of the bodyweight routine. It may take up to four Siren sets to complete one bodyweight set. You now have only two sets to complete, the second shorter in reps. Each set now consists of the following:

Push-ups: 60/40reps
Chin-ups: 30/20 reps
Triceps dips: 60/40 reps
Sit-ups into leg lifts: 60/40 reps
Squats: 100/100 reps
Torso twists: 60/40 reps
Jump rope: 300/200 reps

Remember, 60-30-60-60-100-60-300 for the first set and 40-20-40-40-100-40-200 for the second set. If you finish the second set before finishing your vocal exercises, either continue jumping rope at a slower pace or rest until you have finished your vocal exercises.

DAY 1

MORNING ROUTINE

Start time between 5:00 AM-7:00 AM

Tabata Breathing   ☐
16-ounce water mixture (SVH + DMG)   ☐
One dropperful each of Sinus Clear Out + DMG   ☐
Five Rites- Twenty-one reps each   ☐
VSR/VSP/Voice RX Warm up   ☐

Sirens 1-3-1-5-1-8-1-5-1-3-1
YAH   ☐
YAY   ☐
YEE   ☐
YOH + complete bodyweight routine first set   ☐
YOU   ☐
YAH-AY-EE-OH-OU-AH-AY-EE-OH-OU-AH   ☐
YAY-EE-OH-OU-AH-AY-EE-OH-OU-AH-AY   ☐
YEE-OH-OU-AH-AY-EE-OH-OU-AH-AY-EE + second set   ☐
YOH-OU-AH-AY-EE-OH-OU-AH-AY-EE-OH   ☐
YOU-AH-AY-EE-OH-OU-AH-AY-EE-OH-OU + rest or rope   ☐
Voice & Body Cool Down   ☐

Voice Juice   ☐

DAY 1

AFTERNOON ROUTINE

Start time between 12:00PM-5:00PM

Total Body Cardio- Eight sets ☐
Ultimate Breathing Workout ☐
Bullfrogs- 300 reps ☐
Tongue Pushups- 300 reps ☐

EVENING ROUTINE

60-90 minutes before bedtime

Ultimate Isolation Exercise (Dynamically soft on YEE) ☐
Cardio singing- Sing sixteen songs at full volume ☐
Voice & Body Cool Down ☐

DAY 2

MORNING ROUTINE

Start time between 5:00 AM-7:00 AM

Tabata Breathing ☐
16-ounce water mixture (SVH + DMG) ☐
One dropperful each of Sinus Clear Out + DMG ☐
Five Rites- Twenty-one reps each ☐
VSR/VSP/Voice RX Warm up ☐

Sirens 1-3-1-5-1-8-1-5-1-3-1
YAH ☐
YAY ☐
YEE ☐
YOH + complete bodyweight routine first set ☐
YOU ☐
YAH-AY-EE-OH-OU-AH-AY-EE-OH-OU-AH ☐
YAY-EE-OH-OU-AH-AY-EE-OH-OU-AH-AY ☐
YEE-OH-OU-AH-AY-EE-OH-OU-AH-AY-EE + second set ☐
YOH-OU-AH-AY-EE-OH-OU-AH-AY-EE-OH ☐
YOU-AH-AY-EE-OH-OU-AH-AY-EE-OH-OU + rest or rope ☐
Voice & Body Cool Down ☐

Voice Juice ☐

DAY 2

AFTERNOON ROUTINE

Start time between 12:00PM-5:00PM

Total Body Cardio- Eight sets ☐
Ultimate Breathing Workout ☐
Platysma Pull ups- 80 reps ☐
Head Curls- 80 reps front and back ☐

EVENING ROUTINE

60-90 minutes before bedtime

Ultimate Isolation Exercise (Dynamically soft on YOH) ☐
Cardio singing- Sing sixteen songs at full volume ☐
Voice & Body Cool Down ☐

DAY 3

MORNING ROUTINE

Start time between 5:00 AM-7:00 AM

Tabata Breathing ☐
Mind/Body Process ☐
16-ounce water mixture (SVH + DMG) ☐
Five Rites- Twenty-one reps each ☐
VSR/VSP/Voice RX Warm up ☐

Sirens 1-3-1-5-1-8-1-5-1-3-1
YAH ☐
YAY ☐
YEE ☐
YOH + complete bodyweight routine first set ☐
YOU ☐
YAH-AY-EE-OH-OU-AH-AY-EE-OH-OU-AH ☐
YAY-EE-OH-OU-AH-AY-EE-OH-OU-AH-AY ☐
YEE-OH-OU-AH-AY-EE-OH-OU-AH-AY-EE + second set ☐
YOH-OU-AH-AY-EE-OH-OU-AH-AY-EE-OH ☐
YOU-AH-AY-EE-OH-OU-AH-AY-EE-OH-OU + rest or rope ☐
Voice & Body Cool Down ☐

Voice Juice ☐

DAY 3

AFTERNOON ROUTINE

Start time between 12:00PM-5:00PM

Total Body Cardio- Eight sets ☐
Ultimate Breathing Workout ☐
Bullfrogs- 300 reps ☐
Tongue Pushups- 300 reps ☐

EVENING ROUTINE

60-90 minutes before bedtime

Ultimate Isolation Exercise (Dynamically soft on YOU) ☐
Cardio singing- Sing sixteen songs at full volume ☐
Voice & Body Cool Down ☐

DAY 4

MORNING ROUTINE

Start time between 5:00 AM-7:00 AM

Tabata Breathing   ☐
Mind/Body Process   ☐
16-ounce water mixture (SVH + DMG)   ☐
Five Rites- Twenty-one reps each   ☐
VSR/VSP/Voice RX Warm up   ☐

Sirens 1-3-1-5-1-8-1-5-1-3-1
YAH   ☐
YAY   ☐
YEE   ☐
YOH + complete bodyweight routine first set   ☐
YOU   ☐
YAH-AY-EE-OH-OU-AH-AY-EE-OH-OU-AH   ☐
YAY-EE-OH-OU-AH-AY-EE-OH-OU-AH-AY   ☐
YEE-OH-OU-AH-AY-EE-OH-OU-AH-AY-EE + second set   ☐
YOH-OU-AH-AY-EE-OH-OU-AH-AY-EE-OH   ☐
YOU-AH-AY-EE-OH-OU-AH-AY-EE-OH-OU + rest or rope   ☐
Voice & Body Cool Down   ☐

Voice Juice   ☐

DAY 4

AFTERNOON ROUTINE

Start time between 12:00PM-5:00PM

Total Body Cardio- Eight sets ☐
Ultimate Breathing Workout ☐
Platysma Pull ups- 80 reps ☐
Head Curls- 80 reps front and back ☐

EVENING ROUTINE

60-90 minutes before bedtime

Ultimate Isolation Exercise (Dynamically loud on YAH) ☐
Cardio singing- Sing sixteen songs at full volume ☐
Voice & Body Cool Down ☐

DAY 5

MORNING ROUTINE

Start time between 5:00 AM-7:00 AM

Tabata Breathing   ☐
Mind/Body Process   ☐
16-ounce water mixture (SVH + DMG)   ☐
Five Rites- Twenty-one reps each   ☐
VSR/VSP/Voice RX Warm up   ☐

Sirens 1-3-1-5-1-8-1-5-1-3-1
YAH   ☐
YAY   ☐
YEE   ☐
YOH + complete bodyweight routine first set   ☐
YOU   ☐
YAH-AY-EE-OH-OU-AH-AY-EE-OH-OU-AH   ☐
YAY-EE-OH-OU-AH-AY-EE-OH-OU-AH-AY   ☐
YEE-OH-OU-AH-AY-EE-OH-OU-AH-AY-EE + second set   ☐
YOH-OU-AH-AY-EE-OH-OU-AH-AY-EE-OH   ☐
YOU-AH-AY-EE-OH-OU-AH-AY-EE-OH-OU + rest or rope   ☐
Voice & Body Cool Down   ☐

Voice Juice   ☐

DAY 5

AFTERNOON ROUTINE

Start time between 12:00PM-5:00PM

Total Body Cardio- Eight sets ☐
Ultimate Breathing Workout ☐
Bullfrogs- 300 reps ☐
Tongue Pushups- 300 reps ☐

EVENING ROUTINE

60-90 minutes before bedtime

Ultimate Isolation Exercise (Dynamically loud on YAY) ☐
Cardio singing- Sing sixteen songs at full volume ☐
Voice & Body Cool Down ☐

DAY 6

MORNING ROUTINE

Start time between 5:00 AM-7:00 AM

Tabata Breathing ☐
Mind/Body Process ☐
16-ounce water mixture (SVH + DMG) ☐
Five Rites- Twenty-one reps each ☐
VSR/VSP/Voice RX Warm up ☐

Sirens 1-3-1-5-1-8-1-5-1-3-1
YAH ☐
YAY ☐
YEE ☐
YOH + complete bodyweight routine first set ☐
YOU ☐
YAH-AY-EE-OH-OU-AH-AY-EE-OH-OU-AH ☐
YAY-EE-OH-OU-AH-AY-EE-OH-OU-AH-AY ☐
YEE-OH-OU-AH-AY-EE-OH-OU-AH-AY-EE + second set ☐
YOH-OU-AH-AY-EE-OH-OU-AH-AY-EE-OH ☐
YOU-AH-AY-EE-OH-OU-AH-AY-EE-OH-OU + rest or rope ☐
Voice & Body Cool Down ☐

Voice Juice ☐

DAY 6

AFTERNOON ROUTINE

Start time between 12:00PM-5:00PM

Total Body Cardio- Eight sets   ☐
Ultimate Breathing Workout   ☐
Platysma Pull ups- 80 reps   ☐
Head Curls- 80 reps front and back   ☐

EVENING ROUTINE

60-90 minutes before bedtime

Ultimate Isolation Exercise (Dynamically loud on YEE)   ☐
Cardio singing- Sing sixteen songs at full volume   ☐
Voice & Body Cool Down   ☐

REST DAY

We've finally made it past the hump of V30 Extreme, but I'm betting you wish it were Week 5, ha-ha. Relax today and review your accomplishments. What are your ultimate goals with music? Why are you working so hard with V30? There has to be an end goal, and it's time to begin making it happen. You may wish to begin using the Mindset program to program your mind for musical goals such as creative song writing, improving band rehearsals, etc. Now that your voice and body are rockin', it's time to show the world.

Don't forget to warm up. Warm-ups are a part of daily life until you hang up your singing hat. You know how I like to reward you on Week 3, so skip the juice day and have a juicy steak instead. See you in the morning.

V30 EXTREME

WEEK 4

Week 4 continues to increase the reps per each set of the bodyweight routine. It may take up to five or more Siren sets to complete the first bodyweight set. You have only two sets to complete, and the second set has fewer reps. Each set of the bodyweight routine now consists of the following:

Push-ups: 80/20reps
Chin-ups: 40/10 reps
Triceps dips: 80/20 reps
Sit-ups into leg lifts: 80/20 reps
Squats: 150/50 reps
Torso twists: 80/20 reps
Jump rope: 400/100 reps

Remember, 80-40-80-80-150-80-400 for the first set and 20-10-20-20-50-20-100 for the second set. If you finish the second set before finishing all of your Siren sets, continue jumping rope at a slower pace or rest until you've finished your vocal exercises.

DAY 1

MORNING ROUTINE

Start time between 5:00 AM-7:00 AM

Tabata Breathing	☐
Mind/Body Process	☐
16-ounce water mixture (SVH + DMG)	☐
Five Rites- Twenty-one reps each	☐
VSR/VSP/Voice RX Warm up	☐

Sirens 1-3-1-5-1-8-1-5-1-3-1

YAH	☐
YAY	☐
YEE	☐
YOH	☐
YOU + complete bodyweight routine first set	☐
YAH-AY-EE-OH-OU-AH-AY-EE-OH-OU-AH	☐
YAY-EE-OH-OU-AH-AY-EE-OH-OU-AH-AY	☐
YEE-OH-OU-AH-AY-EE-OH-OU-AH-AY-EE	☐
YOH-OU-AH-AY-EE-OH-OU-AH-AY-EE-OH	☐
YOU-AH-AY-EE-OH-OU-AH-AY-EE-OH-OU + second set	☐
Voice & Body Cool Down	☐

Voice Juice	☐

DAY 1

AFTERNOON ROUTINE

Start time between 12:00PM-5:00PM

Total Body Cardio- Nine sets ☐
Ultimate Breathing Workout ☐
Bullfrogs- 400 reps ☐
Tongue Pushups- 400 reps ☐

EVENING ROUTINE

60-90 minutes before bedtime

Ultimate Isolation Exercise (Dynamically loud on YOH) ☐
Cardio singing- Sing eighteen songs at full volume ☐
Voice & Body Cool Down ☐

DAY 2

MORNING ROUTINE

Start time between 5:00 AM-7:00 AM

Tabata Breathing ☐
Mind/Body Process ☐
16-ounce water mixture (SVH + DMG) ☐
Five Rites- Twenty-one reps each ☐
VSR/VSP/Voice RX Warm up ☐

Sirens 1-3-1-5-1-8-1-5-1-3-1
YAH ☐
YAY ☐
YEE ☐
YOH ☐
YOU + complete bodyweight routine first set ☐
YAH-AY-EE-OH-OU-AH-AY-EE-OH-OU-AH ☐
YAY-EE-OH-OU-AH-AY-EE-OH-OU-AH-AY ☐
YEE-OH-OU-AH-AY-EE-OH-OU-AH-AY-EE ☐
YOH-OU-AH-AY-EE-OH-OU-AH-AY-EE-OH ☐
YOU-AH-AY-EE-OH-OU-AH-AY-EE-OH-OU + second set ☐
Voice & Body Cool Down ☐

Voice Juice ☐

DAY 2

AFTERNOON ROUTINE

Start time between 12:00PM-5:00PM

Total Body Cardio- Nine sets ☐
Ultimate Breathing Workout ☐
Platysma Pull ups- 90 reps ☐
Head Curls- 90 reps front and back ☐

EVENING ROUTINE

60-90 minutes before bedtime

Ultimate Isolation Exercise (Dynamically loud on YOU) ☐
Cardio singing- Sing eighteen songs at full volume ☐
Voice & Body Cool Down ☐

DAY 3

MORNING ROUTINE

Start time between 5:00 AM-7:00 AM

Tabata Breathing	☐
Mind/Body Process	☐
16-ounce water mixture (SVH + DMG)	☐
Five Rites- Twenty-one reps each	☐
VSR/VSP/Voice RX Warm up	☐

Sirens 1-3-1-5-1-8-1-5-1-3-1

YAH	☐
YAY	☐
YEE	☐
YOH	☐
YOU + complete bodyweight routine first set	☐
YAH-AY-EE-OH-OU-AH-AY-EE-OH-OU-AH	☐
YAY-EE-OH-OU-AH-AY-EE-OH-OU-AH-AY	☐
YEE-OH-OU-AH-AY-EE-OH-OU-AH-AY-EE	☐
YOH-OU-AH-AY-EE-OH-OU-AH-AY-EE-OH	☐
YOU-AH-AY-EE-OH-OU-AH-AY-EE-OH-OU + second set	☐
Voice & Body Cool Down	☐

Voice Juice	☐

DAY 3

AFTERNOON ROUTINE

Start time between 12:00PM-5:00PM

Total Body Cardio- Nine sets ☐
Ultimate Breathing Workout ☐
Bullfrogs- 400 reps ☐
Tongue Pushups- 400 reps ☐

EVENING ROUTINE

60-90 minutes before bedtime

Ultimate Isolation Exercise (Dynamically soft on YAH) ☐
Cardio singing- Sing eighteen songs at full volume ☐
Voice & Body Cool Down ☐

DAY 4

MORNING ROUTINE

Start time between 5:00 AM-7:00 AM

Tabata Breathing ☐
Mind/Body Process ☐
16-ounce water mixture (SVH + DMG) ☐
Five Rites- Twenty-one reps each ☐
VSR/VSP/Voice RX Warm up ☐

Sirens 1-3-1-5-1-8-1-5-1-3-1
YAH ☐
YAY ☐
YEE ☐
YOH ☐
YOU + complete bodyweight routine first set ☐
YAH-AY-EE-OH-OU-AH-AY-EE-OH-OU-AH ☐
YAY-EE-OH-OU-AH-AY-EE-OH-OU-AH-AY ☐
YEE-OH-OU-AH-AY-EE-OH-OU-AH-AY-EE ☐
YOH-OU-AH-AY-EE-OH-OU-AH-AY-EE-OH ☐
YOU-AH-AY-EE-OH-OU-AH-AY-EE-OH-OU + second set ☐
Voice & Body Cool Down ☐

Voice Juice ☐

DAY 4

AFTERNOON ROUTINE

Start time between 12:00PM-5:00PM

Total Body Cardio- Nine sets ☐
Ultimate Breathing Workout ☐
Platysma Pull ups- 90 reps ☐
Head Curls- 90 reps front and back ☐

EVENING ROUTINE

60-90 minutes before bedtime

Ultimate Isolation Exercise (Dynamically soft on YAY) ☐
Cardio singing- Sing eighteen songs at full volume ☐
Voice & Body Cool Down ☐

DAY 5

MORNING ROUTINE

Start time between 5:00 AM-7:00 AM

Tabata Breathing ☐
Mind/Body Process ☐
16-ounce water mixture (SVH + DMG) ☐
Five Rites- Twenty-one reps each ☐
VSR/VSP/Voice RX Warm up ☐

Sirens 1-3-1-5-1-8-1-5-1-3-1
YAH ☐
YAY ☐
YEE ☐
YOH ☐
YOU + complete bodyweight routine first set ☐
YAH-AY-EE-OH-OU-AH-AY-EE-OH-OU-AH ☐
YAY-EE-OH-OU-AH-AY-EE-OH-OU-AH-AY ☐
YEE-OH-OU-AH-AY-EE-OH-OU-AH-AY-EE ☐
YOH-OU-AH-AY-EE-OH-OU-AH-AY-EE-OH ☐
YOU-AH-AY-EE-OH-OU-AH-AY-EE-OH-OU + second set ☐
Voice & Body Cool Down ☐

Voice Juice ☐

DAY 5

AFTERNOON ROUTINE

Start time between 12:00PM-5:00PM

Total Body Cardio- Nine sets ☐
Ultimate Breathing Workout ☐
Bullfrogs- 400 reps ☐
Tongue Pushups- 400 reps ☐

EVENING ROUTINE

60-90 minutes before bedtime

Ultimate Isolation Exercise (Dynamically soft on YEE) ☐
Cardio singing- Sing eighteen songs at full volume ☐
Voice & Body Cool Down ☐

DAY 6

MORNING ROUTINE

Start time between 5:00 AM-7:00 AM

Tabata Breathing ☐

Mind/Body Process ☐

16-ounce water mixture (SVH + DMG) ☐

Five Rites- Twenty-one reps each ☐

VSR/VSP/Voice RX Warm up ☐

Sirens 1-3-1-5-1-8-1-5-1-3-1

YAH ☐

YAY ☐

YEE ☐

YOH ☐

YOU + complete bodyweight routine first set ☐

YAH-AY-EE-OH-OU-AH-AY-EE-OH-OU-AH ☐

YAY-EE-OH-OU-AH-AY-EE-OH-OU-AH-AY ☐

YEE-OH-OU-AH-AY-EE-OH-OU-AH-AY-EE ☐

YOH-OU-AH-AY-EE-OH-OU-AH-AY-EE-OH ☐

YOU-AH-AY-EE-OH-OU-AH-AY-EE-OH-OU + second set ☐

Voice & Body Cool Down ☐

Voice Juice ☐

DAY 6

AFTERNOON ROUTINE

Start time between 12:00PM-5:00PM

Total Body Cardio- Nine sets ☐
Ultimate Breathing Workout ☐
Platysma Pull ups- 90 reps ☐
Head Curls- 90 reps front and back ☐

EVENING ROUTINE

60-90 minutes before bedtime

Ultimate Isolation Exercise (Dynamically soft on YOH) ☐
Cardio singing- Sing eighteen songs at full volume ☐
Voice & Body Cool Down ☐

REST DAY

We're getting closer to the end of V30 Extreme. I bet you wish you had never signed on for this five-week theater of pain. Too late, you must keep going. Don't give up now. Well, you can give up a little, just for today, because it IS rest day.

As usual, warm up, juice, and rest up, my friend, because tomorrow we start the final week!

V30 EXTREME

WEEK 5

You've made it to the end of the torture. This final week of V30 Extreme will have you at maximum reps per exercises to form one complete set of the bodyweight routine. It doesn't matter how long it takes you to complete the routine, because you are allotted all ten Siren sets to complete your bodyweight routine. Some exercises will take longer than one vocal exercise, while others will flow quicker. It's not a race. The only goal is to complete the bodyweight routine by the time you've finished your vocal exercises. If you finish the bodyweight routine before the vocal exercises, use the time to rest and sip water, but continue to vocalize until the end of the last vocal exercise. The bodyweight routine now consists of the following:

Push-ups: 100 reps
Chin-ups: 50 reps
Triceps dips: 100 reps
Sit-ups into leg lifts: 100 reps
Squats: 200 reps
Torso twists: 100 reps
Jump rope: 500 reps

Remember, 100-50-100-100-200-100-500. Don't forget to use a skip counter and your fingers for counting the reps. Good luck! FYI: I've never made it to this point, ha-ha.

DAY 1

MORNING ROUTINE

Start time between 5:00 AM-7:00 AM

Tabata Breathing ☐
Mind/Body Process ☐
16-ounce water mixture (SVH + DMG) ☐
Five Rites- Twenty-one reps each ☐
VSR/VSP/Voice RX Warm up ☐

Sirens 1-3-1-5-1-8-1-5-1-3-1
YAH ☐
YAY ☐
YEE ☐
YOH ☐
YOU ☐
YAH-AY-EE-OH-OU-AH-AY-EE-OH-OU-AH ☐
YAY-EE-OH-OU-AH-AY-EE-OH-OU-AH-AY ☐
YEE-OH-OU-AH-AY-EE-OH-OU-AH-AY-EE ☐
YOH-OU-AH-AY-EE-OH-OU-AH-AY-EE-OH ☐
YOU-AH-AY-EE-OH-OU-AH-AY-EE-OH-OU + complete set ☐
Voice & Body Cool Down ☐

Voice Juice ☐

DAY 1

AFTERNOON ROUTINE

Start time between 12:00PM-5:00PM

Total Body Cardio- Ten sets ☐
Ultimate Breathing Workout ☐
Bullfrogs- 500 reps ☐
Tongue Pushups- 500 reps ☐

EVENING ROUTINE

60-90 minutes before bedtime

Ultimate Isolation Exercise (Dynamically soft on YOU) ☐
Cardio singing- Sing twenty songs at full volume ☐
Voice & Body Cool Down ☐

DAY 2

MORNING ROUTINE

Start time between 5:00 AM-7:00 AM

Tabata Breathing ☐
Mind/Body Process ☐
16-ounce water mixture (SVH + DMG) ☐
Five Rites- Twenty-one reps each ☐
VSR/VSP/Voice RX Warm up ☐

Sirens 1-3-1-5-1-8-1-5-1-3-1
YAH ☐
YAY ☐
YEE ☐
YOH ☐
YOU ☐
YAH-AY-EE-OH-OU-AH-AY-EE-OH-OU-AH ☐
YAY-EE-OH-OU-AH-AY-EE-OH-OU-AH-AY ☐
YEE-OH-OU-AH-AY-EE-OH-OU-AH-AY-EE ☐
YOH-OU-AH-AY-EE-OH-OU-AH-AY-EE-OH ☐
YOU-AH-AY-EE-OH-OU-AH-AY-EE-OH-OU + complete set ☐
Voice & Body Cool Down ☐

Voice Juice ☐

DAY 2

AFTERNOON ROUTINE

Start time between 12:00PM-5:00PM

Total Body Cardio- Ten sets ☐
Ultimate Breathing Workout ☐
Platysma Pull ups- 100 reps ☐
Head Curls- 100 reps front and back ☐

EVENING ROUTINE

60-90 minutes before bedtime

Ultimate Isolation Exercise (Dynamically loud on YAH) ☐
Cardio singing- Sing twenty songs at full volume ☐
Voice & Body Cool Down ☐

DAY 3

MORNING ROUTINE

Start time between 5:00 AM-7:00 AM

Tabata Breathing	☐
Mind/Body Process	☐
16-ounce water mixture (SVH + DMG)	☐
Five Rites- Twenty-one reps each	☐
VSR/VSP/Voice RX Warm up	☐

Sirens 1-3-1-5-1-8-1-5-1-3-1

YAH	☐
YAY	☐
YEE	☐
YOH	☐
YOU	☐
YAH-AY-EE-OH-OU-AH-AY-EE-OH-OU-AH	☐
YAY-EE-OH-OU-AH-AY-EE-OH-OU-AH-AY	☐
YEE-OH-OU-AH-AY-EE-OH-OU-AH-AY-EE	☐
YOH-OU-AH-AY-EE-OH-OU-AH-AY-EE-OH	☐
YOU-AH-AY-EE-OH-OU-AH-AY-EE-OH-OU + complete set	☐
Voice & Body Cool Down	☐
Voice Juice	☐

DAY 3

AFTERNOON ROUTINE

Start time between 12:00PM-5:00PM

Total Body Cardio- Ten sets ☐
Ultimate Breathing Workout ☐
Bullfrogs- 500 reps ☐
Tongue Pushups- 500 reps ☐

EVENING ROUTINE

60-90 minutes before bedtime

Ultimate Isolation Exercise (Dynamically loud on YAY) ☐
Cardio singing- Sing twenty songs at full volume ☐
Voice & Body Cool Down ☐

DAY 4

MORNING ROUTINE

Start time between 5:00 AM-7:00 AM

Tabata Breathing ☐
Mind/Body Process ☐
16-ounce water mixture (SVH + DMG) ☐
Five Rites- Twenty-one reps each ☐
VSR/VSP/Voice RX Warm up ☐

Sirens 1-3-1-5-1-8-1-5-1-3-1
YAH ☐
YAY ☐
YEE ☐
YOH ☐
YOU ☐
YAH-AY-EE-OH-OU-AH-AY-EE-OH-OU-AH ☐
YAY-EE-OH-OU-AH-AY-EE-OH-OU-AH-AY ☐
YEE-OH-OU-AH-AY-EE-OH-OU-AH-AY-EE ☐
YOH-OU-AH-AY-EE-OH-OU-AH-AY-EE-OH ☐
YOU-AH-AY-EE-OH-OU-AH-AY-EE-OH-OU + complete set ☐
Voice & Body Cool Down ☐

Voice Juice ☐

DAY 4

AFTERNOON ROUTINE

Start time between 12:00PM-5:00PM

Total Body Cardio- Ten sets ☐
Ultimate Breathing Workout ☐
Platysma Pull ups- 100 reps ☐
Head Curls- 100 reps front and back ☐

EVENING ROUTINE

60-90 minutes before bedtime

Ultimate Isolation Exercise (Dynamically loud on YEE) ☐
Cardio singing- Sing twenty songs at full volume ☐
Voice & Body Cool Down ☐

DAY 5

MORNING ROUTINE

Start time between 5:00 AM-7:00 AM

Tabata Breathing ☐
Mind/Body Process ☐
16-ounce water mixture (SVH + DMG) ☐
Five Rites- Twenty-one reps each ☐
VSR/VSP/Voice RX Warm up ☐

Sirens 1-3-1-5-1-8-1-5-1-3-1
YAH ☐
YAY ☐
YEE ☐
YOH ☐
YOU ☐
YAH-AY-EE-OH-OU-AH-AY-EE-OH-OU-AH ☐
YAY-EE-OH-OU-AH-AY-EE-OH-OU-AH-AY ☐
YEE-OH-OU-AH-AY-EE-OH-OU-AH-AY-EE ☐
YOH-OU-AH-AY-EE-OH-OU-AH-AY-EE-OH ☐
YOU-AH-AY-EE-OH-OU-AH-AY-EE-OH-OU + complete set ☐
Voice & Body Cool Down ☐

Voice Juice ☐

DAY 5

AFTERNOON ROUTINE

Start time between 12:00PM-5:00PM

Total Body Cardio- Ten sets ☐
Ultimate Breathing Workout ☐
Bullfrogs- 500 reps ☐
Tongue Pushups- 500 reps ☐

EVENING ROUTINE

60-90 minutes before bedtime

Ultimate Isolation Exercise (Dynamically loud on YOH) ☐
Cardio singing- Sing twenty songs at full volume ☐
Voice & Body Cool Down ☐

DAY 6

MORNING ROUTINE

Start time between 5:00 AM-7:00 AM

Tabata Breathing ☐
Mind/Body Process ☐
16-ounce water mixture (SVH + DMG) ☐
Five Rites- Twenty-one reps each ☐
VSR/VSP/Voice RX Warm up ☐

Sirens 1-3-1-5-1-8-1-5-1-3-1
YAH ☐
YAY ☐
YEE ☐
YOH ☐
YOU ☐
YAH-AY-EE-OH-OU-AH-AY-EE-OH-OU-AH ☐
YAY-EE-OH-OU-AH-AY-EE-OH-OU-AH-AY ☐
YEE-OH-OU-AH-AY-EE-OH-OU-AH-AY-EE ☐
YOH-OU-AH-AY-EE-OH-OU-AH-AY-EE-OH ☐
YOU-AH-AY-EE-OH-OU-AH-AY-EE-OH-OU + complete set ☐
Voice & Body Cool Down ☐

Voice Juice ☐

DAY 6

AFTERNOON ROUTINE

Start time between 12:00PM-5:00PM

Total Body Cardio- Ten sets ☐
Ultimate Breathing Workout ☐
Platysma Pull ups- 100 reps ☐
Head Curls- 100 reps front and back ☐

EVENING ROUTINE

60-90 minutes before bedtime

Ultimate Isolation Exercise (Dynamically loud on YOU) ☐
Cardio singing- Sing twenty songs at full volume ☐
Voice & Body Cool Down ☐

REST DAY

Pat yourself on the back, because if you've actually worked through V30 and V30 Extreme, you are an animal! This was voice and body conditioning at its best.

Take today to rest. In fact, take a few days off, if needed. You deserve it. But don't forget to warm up, and make sure you use today for a juice fast. You can get that juicy steak tomorrow. I know, your mouth is watering, but you can wait another 24 hours. My goal is to instill a once-per-week juice-fasting regimen from this day forward, so no steakie today.

Before I bid you adieu, I want to leave you with one final routine. The V30 Maintenance & Muscle Building routine is a program that will back off all the craziness I just put you through but still present an effective program for maintaining the muscle and vocal range/tone quality you've gained, while making it easier for you to stick to the daily routine. You may wish to print out this diary to reuse it for years to come. Good luck on your journey. As always, keep me updated on your progress by posting on the RYV message board, signing up for our mailing list, and joining the Vendera Vocal Academy at jaimevendera.com.

V30 MAINTENANCE & MUSCLE BUILDING ROUTINE

To save time as well as fine-tune muscle definition, we'll begin splitting the bodyweight routine in half, into an "upper bodyweight routine" and a "lower bodyweight routine," performed on alternate days to allow the muscle groups time to rest and heal.

Each set of the upper bodyweight routine (UBR) consists of:

20 push-ups, 10 chin-ups, 20 dips, and 100 jump ropes. Remember 20, 10, 20, 100.

Each set of the lower bodyweight routine (LBR) consists of:

20 sit-ups into leg lifts, 40 squats, 20 mike-stand twists, and 100 rope jumps. Remember, 20, 40, 20, 100.

There are only five Siren sets for the maintenance program, but we will now add the Ultimate Isolation exercise to the morning routine. I suggest you use either the pure vowel or combination vowel exercises from Week 5 of V30, because the exercises are longer and will give you more time to finish bodyweight sets as well as a longer vocal workout. But you can choose any Siren combination you wish. The afternoon routine will now be optional. I've had many students spend months on the *Ultimate Breathing Workout* or non-vocal exercises, and once they felt they'd reached their goal, they put those exercise routines aside. That is your choice. You can always reinstate the afternoon routine if you want more exercise.

Cardio singing is always a must, but now our goal is 30 to 60 minutes, regardless of how many songs you sing. In addition, Total Body Cardio will be performed at night. Songs can be changed every day. For touring musicians, you may wish to sing your set on the nights you aren't performing. Or you can do some cardio singing on your set list a few hours before the gig. Honestly, gig night won't require cardio singing, because you'll be getting enough cardio singing onstage. But it won't hurt if you do cardio sing before the gig. It will only make you sound better. Weekend warriors used to singing four or five sets of cover tunes on the weekend should consider cardio singing each weeknight on a set that's different from their set list.

This diary consists of only two weeks, which can be repeated indefinitely. The only difference between each week is that one week you'll start the Ultimate Isolation exercise dynamically soft, and the following week you'll start dynamically loud. Again, you may wish to print out the two-week diary to use repeatedly. If you're ready, let's get started.

FIRST WEEK

DAY 1

MORNING ROUTINE

Start time between 5:00 AM-7:00 AM

Tabata Breathing	☐
Mind/Body Process	☐
16-ounce water mixture (SVH + DMG)	☐
Five Rites- Twenty-one reps each	☐
VSR/VSP/Voice RX Warm up	☐

Sirens 1-3-1-5-1-8-1-5-1-3-1

YAH + UBR	☐
YAY + UBR	☐
YEE + UBR	☐
YOH + UBR	☐
YOU + UBR	☐
Ultimate Isolation Exercise (Dynamically soft on YAH)	☐
Voice & Body Cool Down	☐

Voice Juice	☐

DAY 1

AFTERNOON ROUTINE (Optional)

Start time between 12:00PM-5:00PM

Ultimate Breathing Workout ☐
Bullfrogs- 100 reps ☐
Tongue Pushups- 100 reps ☐

EVENING ROUTINE

60-90 minutes before bedtime

Total Body Cardio- Five sets ☐
Cardio singing- Sing 30-60 minutes at full volume ☐
Voice & Body Cool Down ☐

DAY 2

MORNING ROUTINE

Start time between 5:00 AM-7:00 AM

Tabata Breathing	☐
Mind/Body Process	☐
16-ounce water mixture (SVH + DMG)	☐
Five Rites- Twenty-one reps each	☐
VSR/VSP/Voice RX Warm up	☐

Sirens 1-3-1-5-1-8-1-5-1-3-1

YAH + LBR	☐
YAY + LBR	☐
YEE + LBR	☐
YOH + LBR	☐
YOU + LBR	☐
Ultimate Isolation Exercise (Dynamically soft on YAY)	☐
Voice & Body Cool Down	☐
Voice Juice	☐

DAY 2

AFTERNOON ROUTINE (Optional)

Start time between 12:00PM-5:00PM

Ultimate Breathing Workout ☐
Platysma Pull ups- 50 reps ☐
Head Curls- 50 reps front and back ☐

EVENING ROUTINE

60-90 minutes before bedtime

Total Body Cardio- Five sets ☐
Cardio singing- Sing 30-60 minutes at full volume ☐
Voice & Body Cool Down ☐

DAY 3

MORNING ROUTINE

Start time between 5:00 AM-7:00 AM

Tabata Breathing ☐
Mind/Body Process ☐
16-ounce water mixture (SVH + DMG) ☐
Five Rites- Twenty-one reps each ☐
VSR/VSP/Voice RX Warm up ☐

Sirens 1-3-1-5-1-8-1-5-1-3-1
YAH + UBR ☐
YAY + UBR ☐
YEE + UBR ☐
YOH + UBR ☐
YOU + UBR ☐
Ultimate Isolation Exercise (Dynamically soft on YEE) ☐
Voice & Body Cool Down ☐

Voice Juice ☐

DAY 3

AFTERNOON ROUTINE (Optional)

Start time between 12:00PM-5:00PM

Ultimate Breathing Workout   ☐
Bullfrogs- 100 reps   ☐
Tongue Pushups- 100 reps   ☐

EVENING ROUTINE

60-90 minutes before bedtime

Total Body Cardio- Five sets   ☐
Cardio singing- Sing 30-60 minutes at full volume   ☐
Voice & Body Cool Down   ☐

DAY 4

MORNING ROUTINE

Start time between 5:00 AM-7:00 AM

Tabata Breathing   ☐
Mind/Body Process   ☐
16-ounce water mixture (SVH + DMG)   ☐
Five Rites- Twenty-one reps each   ☐
VSR/VSP/Voice RX Warm up   ☐

Sirens 1-3-1-5-1-8-1-5-1-3-1
YAH + LBR   ☐
YAY + LBR   ☐
YEE + LBR   ☐
YOH + LBR   ☐
YOU + LBR   ☐
Ultimate Isolation Exercise (Dynamically soft on YOH)   ☐
Voice & Body Cool Down   ☐

Voice Juice   ☐

DAY 4

AFTERNOON ROUTINE (Optional)

Start time between 12:00PM-5:00PM

Ultimate Breathing Workout   ☐
Platysma Pull ups- 50 reps   ☐
Head Curls- 50 reps front and back   ☐

EVENING ROUTINE

60-90 minutes before bedtime

Total Body Cardio- Five sets   ☐
Cardio singing- Sing 30-60 minutes at full volume   ☐
Voice & Body Cool Down   ☐

DAY 5

MORNING ROUTINE

Start time between 5:00 AM-7:00 AM

Tabata Breathing   ☐
Mind/Body Process   ☐
16-ounce water mixture (SVH + DMG)   ☐
Five Rites- Twenty-one reps each   ☐
VSR/VSP/Voice RX Warm up   ☐

Sirens 1-3-1-5-1-8-1-5-1-3-1
YAH + UBR   ☐
YAY + UBR   ☐
YEE + UBR   ☐
YOH + UBR   ☐
YOU + UBR   ☐
Ultimate Isolation Exercise (Dynamically soft on YOU)   ☐
Voice & Body Cool Down   ☐

Voice Juice   ☐

DAY 5

AFTERNOON ROUTINE

Start time between 12:00PM-5:00PM

Ultimate Breathing Workout ☐
Bullfrogs- 100 reps ☐
Tongue Pushups- 100 reps ☐

EVENING ROUTINE

60-90 minutes before bedtime

Total Body Cardio- Five sets ☐
Cardio singing- Sing 30-60 minutes at full volume ☐
Voice & Body Cool Down ☐

DAY 6

MORNING ROUTINE

Start time between 5:00 AM-7:00 AM

Tabata Breathing	☐
Mind/Body Process	☐
16-ounce water mixture (SVH + DMG)	☐
Five Rites- Twenty-one reps each	☐
VSR/VSP/Voice RX Warm up	☐

Sirens 1-3-1-5-1-8-1-5-1-3-1

YAH + LBR	☐
YAY + LBR	☐
YEE + LBR	☐
YOH + LBR	☐
YOU + LBR	☐
Ultimate Isolation Exercise (Dynamically soft all vowels)	☐
Voice & Body Cool Down	☐

Voice Juice	☐

DAY 6

AFTERNOON ROUTINE (Optional)

Start time between 12:00PM-5:00PM

Ultimate Breathing Workout ☐
Platysma Pull ups- 50 reps ☐
Head Curls- 50 reps front and back ☐

EVENING ROUTINE

60-90 minutes before bedtime

Total Body Cardio- Five sets ☐
Cardio singing- Sing 30-60 minutes at full volume ☐
Voice & Body Cool Down ☐

SECOND WEEK

DAY 1

MORNING ROUTINE

Start time between 5:00 AM-7:00 AM

Tabata Breathing	☐
Mind/Body Process	☐
16-ounce water mixture (SVH + DMG)	☐
Five Rites- Twenty-one reps each	☐
VSR/VSP/Voice RX Warm up	☐

Sirens 1-3-1-5-1-8-1-5-1-3-1

YAH + UBR	☐
YAY + UBR	☐
YEE + UBR	☐
YOH + UBR	☐
YOU + UBR	☐
Ultimate Isolation Exercise (Dynamically loud on YAH)	☐
Voice & Body Cool Down	☐
Voice Juice	☐

DAY 1

AFTERNOON ROUTINE (Optional)

Start time between 12:00PM-5:00PM

Ultimate Breathing Workout ☐
Bullfrogs- 100 reps ☐
Tongue Pushups- 100 reps ☐

EVENING ROUTINE

60-90 minutes before bedtime

Total Body Cardio- Five sets ☐
Cardio singing- Sing 30-60 minutes at full volume ☐
Voice & Body Cool Down ☐

DAY 2

MORNING ROUTINE

Start time between 5:00 AM-7:00 AM

Tabata Breathing   ☐
Mind/Body Process   ☐
16-ounce water mixture (SVH + DMG)   ☐
Five Rites- Twenty-one reps each   ☐
VSR/VSP/Voice RX Warm up   ☐

Sirens 1-3-1-5-1-8-1-5-1-3-1
YAH + LBR   ☐
YAY + LBR   ☐
YEE + LBR   ☐
YOH + LBR   ☐
YOU + LBR   ☐
Ultimate Isolation Exercise (Dynamically loud on YAY)   ☐
Voice & Body Cool Down   ☐

Voice Juice   ☐

DAY 2

AFTERNOON ROUTINE (Optional)

Start time between 12:00PM-5:00PM

Ultimate Breathing Workout ☐
Platysma Pull ups- 50 reps ☐
Head Curls- 50 reps front and back ☐

EVENING ROUTINE

60-90 minutes before bedtime

Total Body Cardio- Five sets ☐
Cardio singing- Sing 30-60 minutes at full volume ☐
Voice & Body Cool Down ☐

DAY 3

MORNING ROUTINE

Start time between 5:00 AM-7:00 AM

Tabata Breathing ☐
Mind/Body Process ☐
16-ounce water mixture (SVH + DMG) ☐
Five Rites- Twenty-one reps each ☐
VSR/VSP/Voice RX Warm up ☐

Sirens 1-3-1-5-1-8-1-5-1-3-1
YAH + UBR ☐
YAY + UBR ☐
YEE + UBR ☐
YOH + UBR ☐
YOU + UBR ☐
Ultimate Isolation Exercise (Dynamically loud on YEE) ☐
Voice & Body Cool Down ☐

Voice Juice ☐

DAY 3

AFTERNOON ROUTINE (Optional)

Start time between 12:00PM-5:00PM

Ultimate Breathing Workout ☐
Bullfrogs- 100 reps ☐
Tongue Pushups- 100 reps ☐

EVENING ROUTINE

60-90 minutes before bedtime

Total Body Cardio- Five sets ☐
Cardio singing- Sing 30-60 minutes at full volume ☐
Voice & Body Cool Down ☐

DAY 4

MORNING ROUTINE

Start time between 5:00 AM-7:00 AM

Tabata Breathing ☐
Mind/Body Process ☐
16-ounce water mixture (SVH + DMG) ☐
Five Rites- Twenty-one reps each ☐
VSR/VSP/Voice RX Warm up ☐

Sirens 1-3-1-5-1-8-1-5-1-3-1
YAH + LBR ☐
YAY + LBR ☐
YEE + LBR ☐
YOH + LBR ☐
YOU + LBR ☐
Ultimate Isolation Exercise (Dynamically loud on YOH) ☐
Voice & Body Cool Down ☐

Voice Juice ☐

DAY 4

AFTERNOON ROUTINE (Optional)

Start time between 12:00PM-5:00PM

Ultimate Breathing Workout ☐
Platysma Pull ups- 50 reps ☐
Head Curls- 50 reps front and back ☐

EVENING ROUTINE

60-90 minutes before bedtime

Total Body Cardio- Five sets ☐
Cardio singing- Sing 30-60 minutes at full volume ☐
Voice & Body Cool Down ☐

DAY 5

MORNING ROUTINE

Start time between 5:00 AM-7:00 AM

Tabata Breathing ☐

Mind/Body Process ☐

16-ounce water mixture (SVH + DMG) ☐

Five Rites- Twenty-one reps each ☐

VSR/VSP/Voice RX Warm up ☐

Sirens 1-3-1-5-1-8-1-5-1-3-1

YAH + UBR ☐

YAY + UBR ☐

YEE + UBR ☐

YOH + UBR ☐

YOU + UBR ☐

Ultimate Isolation Exercise (Dynamically loud on YOU) ☐

Voice & Body Cool Down ☐

Voice Juice ☐

198 | Jaime Vendera

DAY 5

AFTERNOON ROUTINE

Start time between 12:00PM-5:00PM

Ultimate Breathing Workout ☐
Bullfrogs- 100 reps ☐
Tongue Pushups- 100 reps ☐

EVENING ROUTINE

60-90 minutes before bedtime

Total Body Cardio- Five sets ☐
Cardio singing- Sing 30-60 minutes at full volume ☐
Voice & Body Cool Down ☐

DAY 6

MORNING ROUTINE

Start time between 5:00 AM-7:00 AM

Tabata Breathing   ☐
Mind/Body Process   ☐
16-ounce water mixture (SVH + DMG)   ☐
Five Rites- Twenty-one reps each   ☐
VSR/VSP/Voice RX Warm up   ☐

Sirens 1-3-1-5-1-8-1-5-1-3-1
YAH + LBR   ☐
YAY + LBR   ☐
YEE + LBR   ☐
YOH + LBR   ☐
YOU + LBR   ☐
Ultimate Isolation Exercise (Dynamically loud all vowels)   ☐
Voice & Body Cool Down   ☐

Voice Juice   ☐

DAY 6

AFTERNOON ROUTINE (Optional)

Start time between 12:00PM-5:00PM

Ultimate Breathing Workout ☐
Platysma Pull ups- 50 reps ☐
Head Curls- 50 reps front and back ☐

EVENING ROUTINE

60-90 minutes before bedtime

Total Body Cardio- Five sets ☐
Cardio singing- Sing 30-60 minutes at full volume ☐
Voice & Body Cool Down ☐

V30 Q & A

How has your journey been so far? I hope it's been great (and I know it's probably been a wee bit painful.) Before ending, I want to address several questions you may have about V30, to make sure you're well prepared to continue your V30 experience.

What if I miss a day?
As mentioned earlier in the book, if you miss a day or part of a day, you have to repeat that day. At the end of the six-day cycle, you still take a break. If an entire day is missed, it is not counted as your rest day. Repeat the previous day and move on.

What if I'm sick?
I've performed on television shows while dead-dog sick. You CAN do it. Your voice will be fine. The only time you should not vocalize is when you have strep throat or laryngitis, but you already knew this from reading *Raise Your Voice*. Refer to my books for fixer elixir combinations to gargle for a sore throat as well as other vitamins, minerals, herbs, and vocal products to get you through those sick days.

What if my voice is hoarse?
If you wake up with a sore throat, flip through *Voice RX*, to help alleviate your hoarse voice. Another great tip to help heal the cords quicker than lip bubbles is to vocalize on the *Voice RX* warm-up while singing through a straw into a 16–20-ounce bottle of water two-thirds full. You must keep the water bubbling consistently as you vocalize. In *Raise Your Voice* I mention using larger-diameter rubber tubing inserted into a sink of water. The straw is the same concept. By using the straw in water, you put a cap on how much breath can be released. Furthermore, the sound of your voice will reverberate from the water and travel back up the straw and down the trachea to the vocal cords, producing a massaging effect that will begin to help reduce vocal cord swelling.

202 | Jaime Vendera

I heard that vocalizing while doing physical exercise can hurt your voice. Is this true?

No! In fact, studies have shown that chin-ups strengthen the larynx. Performing the bodyweight routine while vocalizing takes your mind off your voice. I've used this concept with singers having trouble with high notes, having them perform jumping jacks or jump on a rebounder while singing. Combining these exercises will make for a fitter, stronger body and voice!

What if I prefer free weights?

That is your choice. If you wish to pack on the muscle, then you may need a more intense approach as opposed to bodyweight exercises. I suggest using free-weight exercises or exercise machines that will work the same muscle group as each bodyweight exercise in the same order. You must always use the jump rope.

Should I continue voice juice and juice fasting?

Absolutely! In fact, there is nothing wrong with juicing every day. I'm not saying you need to live on juice, but make juicing part of your diet by drinking juice with a meal or replacing one meal with juice. Review *Raise Your Voice* and *Superior Vocal Health* to learn more about what you can do to live a healthier life by choosing better foods and using appropriate supplements.

I'm having trouble with some of the physical exercises. What should I do?

Been there! So, I understand. I have had shoulder and ankle issues which caused me to alter some exercises when needed. I've performed push-ups with my knees touching the mat, even substituted reverse Lat pulldowns for chin-ups. With a little research, you can alter each exercise if you're physically unable to perform the exercise as described in this book. As well, if you feel an exercise is becoming too easy, there are ways to make it more challenging. You can incorporate a kettlebell swing between your legs for squats, wear ankle/wrist weights, etc. Bottom line; don't let it stress you out. Adapt as needed.

Can I add other exercises?

Once you've completed V30, you can add other physical or vocal exercises, even if you decide to go on to V30 Extreme or the V30 Maintenance & Muscle Building Routine. These include routines such as Treadmill Speed Alternating as explained in *Raise Your Voice 2* (I sometimes add this in the morning right before VSR/VSP) or advanced breathing exercises from *The Ultimate Breathing Workout*, as well as grit exercises from my *Extreme Scream* programs and scales such as *Jim Gillette's Vocal Power*. I also approve of adding routines from any coaches published through Vendera Publishing, such as Ray West, James Lugo, Valerie Bastien, and Elizabeth Sabine. My other top coach is Thomas Appell. By following the guidance of Thomas, Jim, and Elizabeth, I developed my own voice, so I fully support them.

It's called SingFit, but where's the singing?

You CAN substitute singing songs for the mini-Sirens, but ONLY after you've finished the five-week program. Simply turn on your favorite tunes and have at it!

I'm in Week 3, but I just can't reach my highest note. What should I do?

SingFit isn't a race; don't fret if there are a few mid-range notes you haven't mastered as you go through the weeks. Regardless of the week, whether Week 1 or Week 5, continue to build your scale based around your point of reference and continue using it. Allow the scale to play to the end and just listen to the notes as you do the physical exercises. In time, all the notes will be easy.

I'm pressed for time; can I combine all the daily routines?

Listen, I'm there with you, as I like to knock things out. If you're tough enough to do it and you want to knock out all three routines in the morning, afternoon, or evening because of time constraints, that is your call. It's best done as the daily program calls for, but you can combine. If you do, I suggest combining the morning and afternoon routines in the morning and leave the evening by itself. Again, that is your call. Just finish everything on the list. Just so you know, there have been weeks when I did the morning and afternoon routines plus cardio singing and performed Total Body Cardio and Isolation exercises in the evening and it all worked out fine.

I just can't seem to do V30 six times a week. Should I give up?

Absolutely not! Turn V30 into a ten-week program. Spend two weeks covering each week in the program, performing the daily routine every other day (for example, Monday, Wednesday, Friday).

I'm in great shape and I already work out religiously. Can I skip the first two weeks of the V30 program?

Do NOT skip any of the weeks, even if you're comfortable with your lower range, or are used to doing more exercise. The first weeks of this program begin a progressive growth state, leading you toward more-intense workouts and programming you to stick to the routine. Start slow and you will grow!

I either finish my exercises first or my vocalizing first. How do I get them close to ending at the same time?

As I said earlier, you simply finish the scale and all reps of your exercises per set, regardless of whether the scales end first or the bodyweight exercises end first. However, if you use my app TUNED XD, you can change the speed of the scales by changing the tempo in the metronome settings to even out the set.

What about diet?

Training cannot overcome poor nutrition, so you need to follow some sort of "singer's diet." If you've read *Raise Your Voice*, you know that white salt, white flour, and white sugar are bad for singers. Caffeine, alcohol, OTC drugs, smoking, and (for some) dairy products can wreak havoc on the voice and body. You're also familiar with the Gracie Diet and the diet in Thomas Appell's book *Never Get Another Cold.* I'm not a diet expert, and, except for juice fasting and my own personal eating habits, I wasn't thinking about a diet plan consisting of healthy proteins, fruits, and veggies, etc., as I wrote this book. Your diet must come from you.

Therefore, YES, you MUST eat healthy and focus on better eating habits, eliminating bad food from your regimen. Please do some research and decide what eating habits are best for you.

Do I REALLY have to do ten vocal/exercise sets?

Yes, if you want results! Have you ever noticed when working out that your muscles do become fatigued with each passing set, but you also feel more heat rising off your body, more blood pumping through your veins, and more energy pulsating through your body? The harder you work, the more gains you'll make. A similar thing is happening with your voice. With each passing vocal set, the energy is rising and the blood is pumping. However, if you apply correct vocal technique, you won't feel that muscle tiredness as you're doing your sets. Instead, you'll feel vocal elated, as if you're entering a state of vocal Nirvana. Your first set of vowels might sound a bit dry, weak, or wispy. By set ten, your tone is effortless, strong, and resonant. The reason-your hard work! So, do the sets as described.

I hope you've enjoyed this crazy ride. Now, if you'll excuse me, I've got some bodyweight exercises to perform, some students to teach, some shows to film, and more books to write, ha-ha. C-ya soon!

ABOUT THE AUTHOR

Glass shattering vocal coach and honorary MythBuster, Jaime Vendera is quickly becoming one of the most sought-after vocal coaches on the planet. Using his own methods (Vocal Stress Release and the Isolation method) Jaime turned his two-octave range into multiple octaves with over 120 decibels of raw vocal power. When singers need more vocal range, power, and stamina, and need to maintain their voices night after night, they call Jaime Vendera. Jaime is the author of well over a dozen books, most noted, *Raise Your Voice*, which is used by some of the top singers in the world, including Myles Kennedy (Alter Bridge/Slash) who has personally told Jaime that he keeps a copy of *Raise Your Voice* with him on tour. A few of Jaime's students include James LaBrie (Dream Theater), Terry Ilous (XYZ, Great White), Kevin Rudolf, Clayton Stroope (Thriving Ivory/Midnight Cinema) and many more.

What singers say about Jaime:

*Jaime is the 'Mr. Miyagi' of vocal coaches- Ben Thomas of Zappa Plays Zappa

*Jaime is the 'Yoda.' of vocal training- Mat Devine of Kill Hannah

*Because of my lessons with Jaime, my voice is feeling and sounding better than it has in twenty years. I am spot-on every night. He is the Vocal Guru- James LaBrie of Dream Theater

*One time during a tour, I was so sick I could barely make it through the set. It looked as if we were going to have to cancel the next show. Jaime spent some time giving me some tips that helped me regain my voice. By the next night, I was able to perform the show. He is fantastic! Raise Your Voice Second Edition is THE book for singers. I keep it on tour with me. I recommend his book and his private instruction to ALL singers- Myles Kennedy of Alter Bridge

*I am hitting notes on tour that I forgot I had thanks to Jaime Vendera- Terry Ilous of Great White/XYZ